Lightning Learning

A Brain Training Programme that will accelerate your Learning & Thinking through the 21st century

Jonathan O'Brien

Cartoons by Ash

A QUANTUM Publication

First published in Great Britain in 1996. reprinted and re edited 1997, 1998, 1999, 2000

Latest Edition 2004

Copyright 2005 Jonathan and Brenda O'Brien, The Great Little Book Company

A Great Little Book Company Ltd Publication
The moral right of the author has been asserted.
ALL RIGHTS RESERVED

No part of this publication may be reproduced, in any form or by any means (including seminars, workshops, training programmes, classes, etc.), without prior permission in writing of the publisher, nor be otherwise circulated in any form of binding or cover other than that which it is published and without a similar condition including this condition being imposed on the subsequent purchaser.
Readers are strongly encouraged and advised where necessary, and if in doubt, to seek professional advice (i.e. doctor in relation to diet and exercise). Quantum UK Ltd and the Great Little Book Company Ltd, (The Quantum Group) cannot be held responsible for any claim for death, bodily injury and so forth occuring in connection with this publication (other than such damage caused by the negligence of the Quantum Training Group).

©JP & BA O'Brien, The Great Little Book Company – 3rd Edition 2004
Designed and Produced by Admor Ltd
Published by The Great Little Book Company Ltd, PO Box 31, Chichester West Sussex PO18 8BQ
Tel: 01243 572132 Fax: 01243 573151

THE LIBRARY, SPARSHOLT COLLEGE, HAMPSHIRE

ACCESSION No: 036409   X

CLASS NUMBER: 371.3 OBR

John O'Brien

Acknowledgements:

Thanks to the following who have made the production of this book possible: My wife, Brenda, whose patient and numerous contributions have made the finished product much better than it might otherwise have been. Ashley, whose cartoons bring the words much greater meaning and help to make the book more multi-sensory, Clico and Gerald Kingsbury and family for their support and generosity, Robert and Jane Daniel for their advice and wisdom, Jojo Barnett for her many hours help on the word processor, Louise Burston and the many colleagues and students, both old and young, who have contributed advice and personal experience and to whom this book is dedicated and to Stephen Hajnal - Smith and his team for help with production and the many others who have proof read the current edition. Thanks again to Brenda - always patient and quick with bright ideas!

As our understanding of the learning process continues to expand and further amendments and changes in this text take place, thanks must also go to the team at the Quantum Thinking Learning & Development Centre, in Sussex and particularly to Libby Wing who looks after the Great Little Book Company Ltd.

(August 2004)

About the author:

Jonathan O'Brien is an educational and management consultant and a former Director of Studies and Housemaster with many years experience in both the educational and commercial world. Over the last ten years, Quantum Training UK Ltd has been his main focus, and more recently he has concentrated upon the Great Little Book Company Ltd (formerly Quantum Publishing) and the newly opened Quantum Training Learning Development Centre is Bosham, Sussex.

His particular interest is in working towards an educational system that prepares individuals fully for the "outside world" and the many opportunities that lie ahead.

Other titles include:	Lightning Learning II (KS 2) (GLB Co. Ltd) (Brenda O'Brien)
	Lightning Learning III (KS 3) (GLB Co. Ltd)
	Brain Trainer (Longman)
	Brain Trainer Advanced (Longman)
	Great Little Book of Brainpower (GLB Co. Ltd)
	Great Little Book of Showing You Know (GLB Co. Ltd)

Forthcoming titles in 2004 and 2005:	The Great Little Book of Sport on the Brain
	The Great Little Book of Positive Success
	The Great Little Book of Coaching

Foreword

THE LIBRARY, SPARSHOLT COLLEGE, HAMPSHIRE

ACCESSION No: 036409

CLASS NUMBER:

Why ?

There are many texts on the market that deal with Study Skills and Accelerated Learning - but there are not many that explain in a holistic manner just how individuals can help themselves to Train their own Brains. We hope that this will be useful as a self-study text as well as a book that can be used in the classroom to help students learn the essential skills of how to learn. It will be useful especially for anyone approaching exams and for those in need of more focus, confidence and motivation when approaching coursework at Secondary Level.

This latest edition brings additional information and up-to-date research.

Throughout the text this cartoon brain power "BP" will illustrate some of the points we make and hopefully keep you amused!

Lightening Learning, and the abridged version "The Great Little Book of Brainpower", have proved very popular with students over the last eight years, principally, it seems, because it is uncomplicated and easy to use. I am encouraged by this, as at outset any intention was to help students cope with the difficulties of academic pressures and to optimise personal learning using the whole of their brain.

There has been a temptation to submerge students in the latest research and developments into the brain and metacognitive understanding: I have tried to keep the theoretical explanation to a minimum, if I have over-simplified or inadvertantly made errors then I hope they will forgive me in the interests of their own improved success.

Jon O'Brien

August 2004

Dedication:
To Toby

The Lightning Learning Process

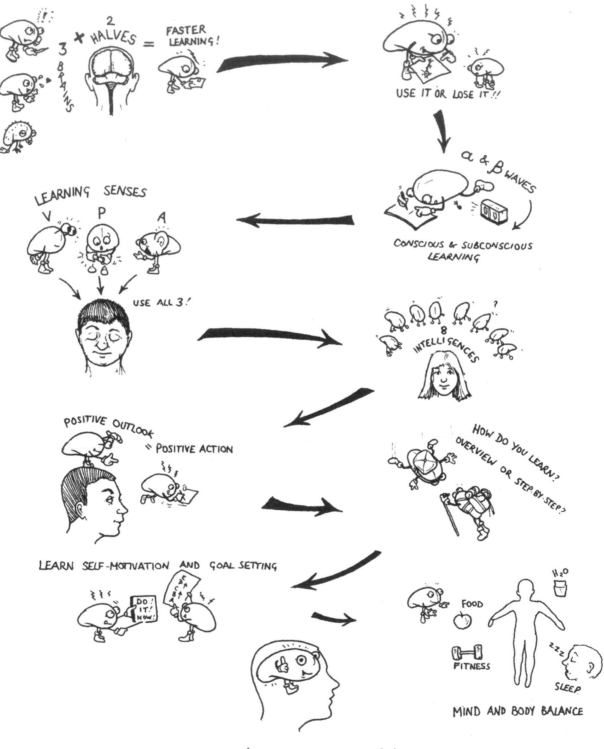

An Overview

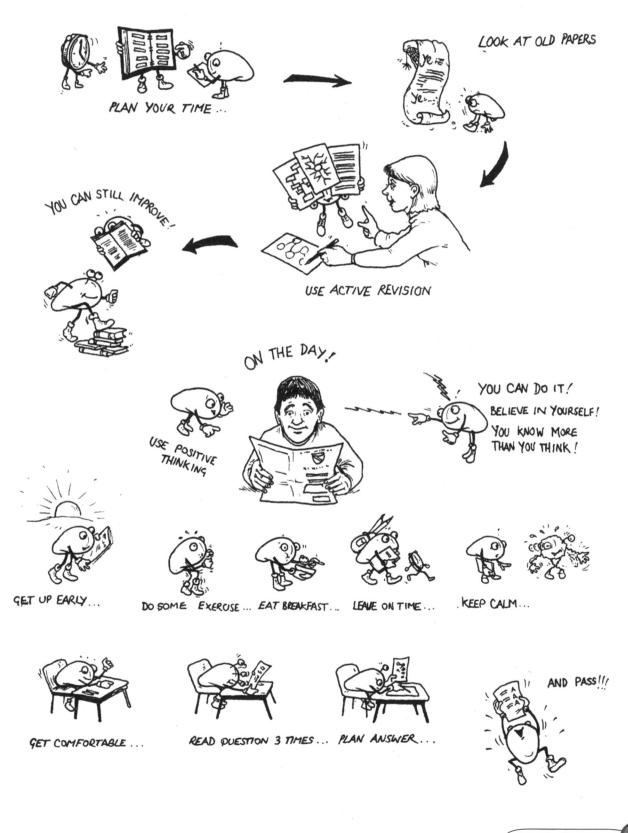

PLAN YOUR TIME...

LOOK AT OLD PAPERS

USE ACTIVE REVISION

YOU CAN STILL IMPROVE!

ON THE DAY!

USE POSITIVE THINKING

YOU CAN DO IT!
BELIEVE IN YOURSELF!
YOU KNOW MORE
THAN YOU THINK!

GET UP EARLY...

DO SOME EXERCISE... EAT BREAKFAST... LEAVE ON TIME...

KEEP CALM...

GET COMFORTABLE...

READ QUESTION 3 TIMES... PLAN ANSWER...

AND PASS!!!

Contents
Seven Steps
of Lightning Learning

Use your head
to get ahead

Lightning Learning

What is Lightning Learning ?

Lightning Learning is about YOU and how you can become an Enlightened Learner – it's about how you can change your life...and with no extra effort!

Learning is not merely about what you are taught – facts and information. Information and facts can be put in front of you, but what you do with it, how much you convert to knowledge remember and apply successfully – perhaps in exams or other situations, is UP TO YOU !

This book will help you become more successful in your forthcoming exams and also equip you with skills you will need for the rest of your life .

It will teach you about HOW you learn and introduce you to a number of Smarter Studying Techniques which you can apply to any task, project or learning situation.

Studying and Learning can become easier and faster, more enjoyable, more rewarding, less stressful and help you achieve better results.

You can become more organised, more positive, more confident, more self -disciplined, more self - empowered and more SUCCESSFUL!

Facts about Learning:

Learning is about how your brain takes in, interprets, records and stores information .

It is about how you connect up the 100 billion brain cells in your brain to make a unique network of pathways which is known as your 'unique cognitive map'.

It does not just happen in a classroom or for exams and does not stop when you leave school or university. It is something which happens all around you for the rest of your life.

Learning can be both conscious and sub-conscious. But conscious learning requires a the right state of mind and a strategy. It must be active and experienced by you. It is also influenced by attitude, environment and fitness.

Learning is a skill, and learning how to learn is probably one of the more important skills you can acquire.

Everyone can empower themselves to become a good learner.

> You have a chance to choose your future in a way that you probably haven't realised that you can. The Lightning Learning programme can help you achieve it.

and Brain Training Skills

This book could change the way you learn and study, as well as change your attitudes about learning and studying and even change your future and your expectations.

**BUT ... only if you want it to.
It's your life, your success, your responsibility**

You need to:

Actively participate by contributing to this text.

Answer the questions, have a go at the action tasks

Add your own ideas .....even use it as a 'scribble pad' while you're thinking.

Try out the ideas in your daily routine.

Believe you can, and you will improve.

Use all your intelligences

Form your own customised learning / working style.

HOW do I use this book?

● **STEP 1**

Skim through each section before you read it throughly.

Look at the Quantum Leap objectives at the beginning of each section

Look at the Overview Brain Frame at the end of each section.

● **STEP 2**

Read it section by section and sub-section by sub-section.

Scribble, annotate, try out the exercises.

● **STEP 3**

Highlight specific areas of benefit. Note what works for you.

Its about **how** you learn and not just what you learn

● **STEP 4**

Look at the Overview Brain Frame again.

● **STEP 5**

Create your own action plan and

prefered learning procedure.

* IDEA...Listen to gentle, non-lyrical music while you're doing it - colour in, scribble, highlight ... relax and try it!

How good is your Brain and Learning?

Yes · Sometimes · Rarely · Never

Question	Yes	Sometimes	Rarely	Never
Do you know how to make yourself work, even when you really don't want to?	○	○	○	○
Do you organise your day, work and free time, so everything is done on time?	○	○	○	○
Do you listen carefully in class and do you know how to concentrate better?	○	○	○	○
Do you use different strategies to learn facts and remember them under pressure?	○	○	○	○
Do you make efficient, easy to remember notes, using key ideas or facts only?	○	○	○	○
Do you understand what the question is asking?	○	○	○	○
Do you know your strongest learning style?	○	○	○	○
Do you know how to use different resources and how to select important information?	○	○	○	○
Do you ask yourself why you're studying a topic?	○	○	○	○
Are you selective about what you read rather than waste time reading large chunks?	○	○	○	○
Do you make notes using key facts and ideas only without every detail?	○	○	○	○
Do you approach revision and exams in a positive and confident way?	○	○	○	○
Do you organise your notes and files so you know where everything is?	○	○	○	○
Do you make a revision timetable at least 4 weeks before the exams?	○	○	○	○
Do you plan different ways to learn and understand a topic?	○	○	○	○
Do you know how to work under pressure in an exam?	○	○	○	○
Do you see learning and school as a "stepping stone' leading to a great future?	○	○	○	○
Do you believe in yourself, think positively and remain confident?	○	○	○	○
Do you want to be successful, in control of your life?	○	○	○	○

Marking

More than 18 "Yes"
A. outstanding. Brillant you don't need to read this book!
B. You're a liar!

More than 10 "Yes/Sometimes"
Good - but read on, you'll learn something new

More than 10 "Rarely/Never"
Not bad.. this book, your commitment and your teachers will help you improve

More than 15 "Nevers"
All is not lost if you start to change now. This book is definitely for you!

Notes

Brain Power: The Benefits

YOU WILL:

- have a larger faster memory
- improve your problem solving skills
- increase your own motivation as your realise these skills are improving your results
- become more positive
- feel in control of your life and learning
- feel less worried and more reassured about your learning
- learn how to organise everything you have to do and want to do
- gain heightened confidence and a 'feel good' factor!
- find your tasks become easier to do and more interesting
- learn to have a stronger mind-power
- learn to reach 'peak-performance'
- discover hidden intelligences

Please take a moment to read through the above list and choose *two* that make a particular impact on you, and that you would especially like to possess as a result of this working book on your brain. Write them both (or more) below:

_____

_____

_____

_____

_____

_____

Your Unique Ability

The First Leap will introduce you to how your brain works and how you take in information and convert it into knowledge.

These are vital ingredients in improvement of your learning.

Once you know how your brain works best and know how its is 'wired', you will be able to customise your own learning strategies and be able to think, understand and memorise faster.

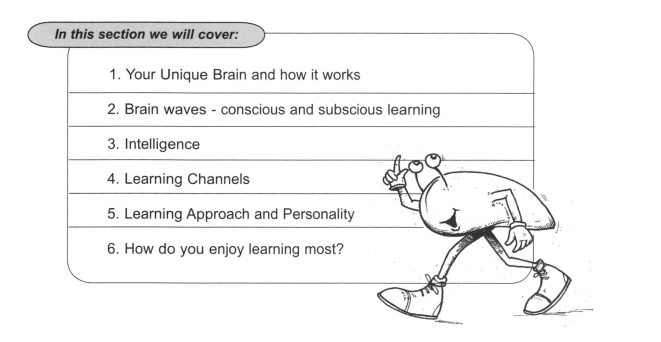

In this section we will cover:

1. Your Unique Brain and how it works

2. Brain waves - conscious and subscious learning

3. Intelligence

4. Learning Channels

5. Learning Approach and Personality

6. How do you enjoy learning most?

Notes

You have a unique brain!

Your Unique Brain

You have billions of brain cells capable of making a hundred billion connections, processing 1,000 new pieces of information every second. Learning takes place when brain cells make connections. You can make more connections than there are atoms in the universe! They form a vast network of knowledge and experience.

This is how it works:

Your brain passes messages between brain cells linking them to make pathways everytime you have a thought or an experience. Sensations or 'messages' are received from your senses - sounds, visual images, tastes, touch and movement.

The messages travel along these pathways as electrical impulses (or brain waves) to different parts of the brain where they are processed to become meaningful.

Different parts of the brain are designed to process different information.

The greater number of thoughts or experiences you have, the greater the number of connections you will make in your brain and the more of your brain will be used.

When thoughts and experiences are new, the connections are weak and the information travels slowly. The task you are doing appears difficult. But the more often you practice and repeat the same thing, the stronger the connections become and the faster the information travels around your brain. Brain cells are coated in Myelin, a waxy substance; they are thicker and information can travel along them faster. It's the difference between a country road and a motorway! Practice is what makes learning and doing a particular task more easy and eventually automatic.

You need many brain and strong brain cell connections.
Thicker brains are good!

Intelligence is not FIXED

Intelligence or IQ is about how many of your brain cells are connected to each other and how fast the electrical impulses travel between them.

Therefore the more experiences you have, the more you learn and the greater number of ways you explore the same topic, the more connections you make, the 'bigger' your brain becomes *and the more intelligent you become.*

You can increase the number of connections by using your multi intelligences.

Your multiple brain:

Each area of the brain is responsible for specific functions and can be divided

into various parts or 'brains'.

A Simple Brain or 'Reptilian' (Hindbrain)

Deals with involuntary functions such as breathing and

heartbeat or pulse rate and reacts to the basic stimuli

- danger, fear, shelter, protection, anxiety and safety. It horses

also the Celebellum.

A Middle or 'Mammalian' Brain (Midbrain)

Deals with your emotions, mood, feelings, concentration and

learning ability. It is where your long term memory is located and regulated.

It is made up of the Tharmus and the Hypotralmus.

A Higher Thinking Brain or 'Forebrain' (Cerebral Cortex)

80% of the whole brain. Deals with conscious thought and learning, sight,

hearing, co-ordination, touch, language, thinking, problem solving, making

decisions and so on.

It processes information coming in from all over our body.

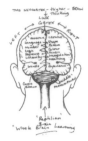

Your Two Halves:

The 'Higher' Brain is split into two 'hemispheres', one on the right side ... one on the left.

The two hemispheres have different functions, broadly speaking, but these are not exclusively different. It's a generalisation, though, this is useful to you in explaining how using both hemispheres during one learning task will help you learn faster.

Left Hemisphere

Speech and Words

Numbers

Symbols / Sequences

Facts and Detail

Writing

Processes parts to make the whole
"Conscious Learning"

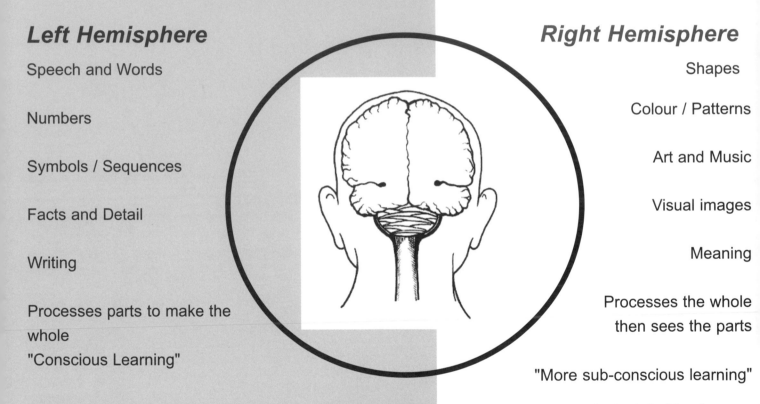

Right Hemisphere

Shapes

Colour / Patterns

Art and Music

Visual images

Meaning

Processes the whole
then sees the parts

"More sub-conscious learning"

The left hemisphere controls the right side of the body and the right hemisphere controls the left side of the body. They are joined by a mass of nerve fibres called the Corpus Callosum and messages are passed across from one side to the other. Most people tend to have a more developed hemisphere. Those of us with a more dominant left hemisphere will be better at arithmetic and written language, where as those with a more developed right hemisphere will tend to be more artistic, musical and good at spatial subjects like Design Technology and Geometry.

What has become very clear is that, by employing tasks which link both Left and Right Hemispheres simultaneously, we learn better, faster and have more fun!

Brain Waves

CONSCIOUS AND SUB CONSCIOUS LEARNING

Brain Waves work on 4 frequencies and are the electric impulses that travel along brain cells, passing messages to each other.

BETA Conscious, alert, active waves

ALPHA Sub-conscious waves, relaxed but alert

THETA Deep meditation. Dreaming brainwaves. Very creative. Active before deep sleep or just before waking.

DELTA Deep sleep waves

CONSCIOUS LEARNING

When you are reading, writing and concentrating you are using BETA WAVES and processing information in your left hemisphere.

SUB-CONSCIOUS LEARNING

Sub-conscious learning happens mainly through your right hemisphere when you are relaxed and your ALPHA BRAIN WAVES are buzzing.

Have you ever wondered why you can remember the words of a song or TV advertisement when you did not actually sit down and learn them?

90 % OF YOUR LEARNING IS:

Sub-Conscious Learning.
Sub-Conscious Learning.
Sub-Conscious Learning.
Sub-Conscious Learning.

Surf Your brain waves!

Remember the best way to learn is when Right and Left hemispheres work simultaneously - so the Alphas and Betas are both buzzing !

TIPS TO GET THE ALPHAs AND BETAs BUZZING

1. Play low volume, non lyrical, classical music (60 beats per minute) when you are studying and concentrating.

2. Make and play a game using all the facts you need to know for each subject.

3. Make colourful posters or drawings of all the facts you need to know and hang them around your room (Like advertising Bill boards).

4. Record the facts you need to know onto tape and play it when you are travelling to school or apparently relaxing.

5. Doodle or use a highlighter pen as you read and revise.

6. Relate all new facts to a pleasant experience

7. Create pictures of learning in your Mind's eye

Keep cool, stay relaxed, *believe*

LEARNING WHILE YOU ARE ASLEEP

THETA WAVES are those which occur during "dream time" or Rapid Eye Movement time when you are asleep, thought to be about 20% of total sleep time. The brain uses this time to sort out information that has come in during the day and file it away. You will tend to remember information that you have scanned or listened to on tape just before going to sleep. You may also find you wake up with the solution to a problem you've been puzzling over.

Sub-conscious Learning - You Learn without realising it!

Using your Whole Brain

The Parts Make a Whole

It's also important to understand Learning is not just about what is happening in your Thinking Brain but is affected by the state of your BODY and MIND. The various parts of your brain, Reptilian, Mammalian and Thinking Brain all work together and influence your Learning. If you become stressed or anxious, your Reptilian Brain takes over restricts clear thinking and access to memory in the rest of your brain. You may experience uncontrollable symptoms like "butterflies", rapid heartbeat or sickness.

Being Relaxed is Essential to Learning

All in-coming information passes through the Mammalian Brain (which controls emotion, attitude, mood and immune system) on its way to the Thinking Brain. So if you are in a good mood and feel confident and happy, the information will enter easily. If you are upset, tired, hungry and feel negative about what you are learning, the information will be either rejected or stored as an unpleasant memory.

Being Positive is Essential to Learning

The left hemisphere processes more academic information, the right hemisphere processes more creative information. Learning is increased by about 300% when both hemispheres work together - for instance when using colour and pictures with facts and logical steps

Using Both Hemispheres Together Increases Learning

Notes

Understanding the Learning Process

Discover how you learn.

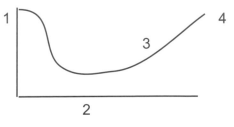

THERE ARE FOUR PHASES

1. We are unaware of how much we know or need to know
2. We realise we need to know more. Confidence drops
3. Increase your ability - Confidence increases
4. Ability & confidence are high. Move on to the next learning challenge - it will follow the same pattern

Not sure how Much we know...

Phase 1

Now we know we know !

Phase 4

We begin to know...

Now we know we don't know...

Phase 2

Phase 3

The Phases of Learning

THE FIVE STEPS OF LEARNING - the 4 M's

Maximising
· Brainpower is increased through the self knowledge of multi-sensory learning, learning personality and multiple intelligences.

Mindpower
· Focus your mind on why you are learning - the purpose
· Positive state of mind

Management
· Plan your time, use brainframes, read according to need, choose resourses
· Break your learning down into manageable chunks
· Prepare kit, resources, environment and sessions

Memorising
· Intend to learn
· Multi - sense data into your brain

Making Sure
· Show you know
· Reflect upon this for the next time

MANAGING BRAIN POWER

5 M's of LEARNING

MIND STATE

MANUFACTURING LEARNING

MEMORISING & REVIEWING

MAKE SURE YOU KNOW

YOU HAVE AT LEAST 9 MULTI SENSORY INTELLIGENCES - probably more!

Intelligence can also be defined as Methods of Thinking and Doing.

1.	*LINGUISTIC*	- Talking, Writing, Reading.
2.	*MATHEMATICAL/LOGICAL*	- Numbers. Systems, Logical thought, Problem solving
3.	*VISUAL/SPATIAL*	- How things look. Imagination. Creating images. Using Space
4.	*TACTILE/PHYSICAL*	- Doing, building, touching, moving (Sports, Dancing...)
5.	*MUSICAL*	- Melody, rhythm, playing music, singing, creating tunes.
6.	*INTERPERSONAL*	- Communicating well with others. Rapport.
7.	*INTRAPERSONAL*	- Talking positively, to yourself. Self-analysis. Being objective.
8.	*INTUITIVE*	- Perceiving information not available to the "senses".
9.	*CREATIVE*	- Finding new solutions, new ideas
10.	*NATURALISTIC*	- Having a strong awareness of environment and nature.

These intelligences are also talents. All intelligences are equally important. Using all your intelligences will increase your capacity for learning and help you to find solutions from all angles. This is a particularly valuable life skill. In Quantum Leap 3, you will be shown how to use all your intelligences to explore a specific task and learn in a Multi-Sensory, 'whole-brain' way.

Your Learning Channels

This is how to take in information best !

All information is taken in through your senses and transmitted to your brain for processing and interpretation. Most people have a preferred way of taking in information and learning.

Your Multi Sensory Channels

You have five senses, and you can learn and remember using all of them. Sound, sight and touch are the more dominant senses for learning channel. Taste and smell are minor for academic learning, but they can be directly associated with positive or negative feelings about learning.

If you know your preferred Channel you can adapt the way you study to the way you learn best. Use your strongest channel to compensate for your weaker channels.

VISUAL LEARNERS

You learn through SEEING things in your "Mind's Eye". Perhaps through 'images', diagrams, pictures, metaphors, analogies or similies – if you are not sure what these are.......ASK someone.

AUDITORY LEARNERS

You learn through processing sounds – listening in class, you can remember well by HEARING the lesson. You will learn well from audio tapes and conversations. It also is about talking to yourself. It's through your "Mind's Ear".

PHYSICAL LEARNERS

PRACTICAL: You learn well by becoming physically involved in 'doing' something. TACTILE: Touch. Rough or smooth, how it 'feels' in your mind.... Perhaps when you're designing a project, or when you're writing a descriptive essay or story.

It's also important to realise that you can and should try to use as many senses as you can. It doubles or trebles learning ability!

We learn through **all** our **senses**, so you can't leave any out. The best way to learn is using them all.

We remember:

20% of what we hear

30% of what we say

40% of what we see

50% of what we do

and **90%** of what we **see hear say and do**

Typical V.A.P. Characteristics

VISUAL PEOPLE

Plan ahead with timetable

Like detail

Like to look good

Spell well

Remember by visual imagery

Fast readers

Fast speakers

Don't listen well

Like pictorial lessons

Like an overall view

Draw, scribble, doodle

Like tidy work

Prefer to do rather than speak

Prefer 'Art' to 'Music'

Daydream often

Prefer cartoons

Like metaphors/similes

"That looks right to me"

"I can see what you mean"

"I CAN PICTURE THE SCENE".

"It's crystal clear in my mind"

"It goes like greased lightning"

AUDITORY PEOPLE

Talk to themselves

Like speeches/singing aloud

Easily distracted by noise

Mouth words

Listen well

Like lessons/lectures

Rhyme & Rhythm are popular

Prefer 'music' to 'art'

Remember by listening

Recall conversations

Chat. Discuss

Argue

Speak well

Tell jokes

Spell out loud

Don't visualise well

Understand verbal instructions

"I hear what you're saying"

"That rings a bell"

"Sounds great to me"

"I tune in to your thoughts"

PHYSICAL/PRACTICAL PEOPLE

Move a lot

Like Physical activity

Make/alter things

Remember by doing/undoing

Use gestures

Fidget

Need to visit a place to remember it

Like action words/descriptions

Like close proximity

Speak quite slowly

"Let's tackle the issue"

"Run that by me"

"I'll handle that"

"I feel at home with this idea"

HOW DO YOU ENJOY LEARNING THE MOST ?

Please order in preference	1 (best) 8 (worst)	Reason Advantage/Disadvantage
1 Lessons		
2 Text Book		
3 Video		
4 Audio Tape		
5 Practical/action		
6 Group work/Discussion		
7 Computers		
8 Making notes		

Test Your Senses

Which is your Dominant Learning Sensory Channel?
Please prioritise 1st (top) - 3rd in preference if you can't decide between one and another, give them equal rating...i.e. 1st =

I PREFER TO:	HANDS ON/PRACTICAL	VISUAL	AUDITORY
LEARN	Through practical Activity	With pictures, diagrams, video or by emulating something	By listening - lecture tapes, discussions
SPELL	By writing it out to construct it	By seeing the spelling	By sounding the spelling
WRITE	Action based on paragraphs.	Very descriptive passages	In direct speech, rhyme, rhythm
MEMORISE INFORMATION	By doing/undoing again and again	By imagining in pictures, pattern and colours.	By repeating out loud. Listening. Oral tests. Listening to tapes
UNWIND	By actively "letting off steam"	By watching not doing	By listening i.e. music
COMMUNICATE	By gestures, body language. Reflect mood/ feelings	By watching facial reactions use metaphors, descriptive words and analogies	By detecting mood and information through tone of voice and plenty of listening
READ	Practical/action based material Using context rather than words	See vividly in your mind. By recognising whole words	Speeches, plays, conversation, chatty material
RECALL INFORMATION	By concentrating on action and feelings	Through images, scenes, faces, colour, pattern	By sounding out letters Hearing, sounds, words, stories, examples.
DRAW	Action scenes	Descriptive scenes	Busy, 'noisy' scenes
HEAR	Active material	Descriptive material	Rhythmic, rhymed music, poetry.

Learning Personality Skills

Once you have an idea about your Preferred Learning Channel, you need to consider your... *Learning Personality*

Earlier in the chapter you looked at the skills associated with the left and right hemispheres of your brain . Hemispheric dominance also influences your Learning Personality and the way you approach your work.

Do You Prefer To See the Whole Picture? – The Sky Diver (holistic)

This is the 'Top Down' worker - 'Right brained' - one who sees the answer but can't explain how they worked it out - one who prefers the overview of a subject first. It is the person who likes to work in a random, intuitive way, who thinks in pictures, tends to be non-verbal and fantasy oriented. The sort of person who "can't see the trees from the wood" and who will set out on a journey knowing where they want to go, but not having planned the route .

Do You Prefer To Work Step by Step? – The Intrepid Explorer (sequential)

This is the 'Bottom Up' worker – 'Left brained' – who systematically works out a problem to its conclusion. It is one who likes working with words and symbols, who is logical, sequential and reality based. The sort of person who "can't see the wood from the trees" and who will have planned every detail of a journey before embarking on it.

It's important to understand that no one is completely right hemisphere dominant or completely left hemisphere dominant. And you may approach different subjects in different ways.

You may be good at the more 'left hemisphere' subjects like arithmetic but have a right hemisphere, holistic approach. Or you may be good at right hemisphere typical subjects like art and have a left hemisphere, logical / sequential approach.

What's the Benefit to You?

There are two important reasons for knowing what sort of Learning Personality or Approach you have.

Firstly, it may not be compatible with the way you are being taught. Most teachers tend deliver their lessons in a very logical order. If you are a holistic learner, this step by step way may not suit you – ask for a syllabus or make an overview of the subject so that you can help yourself see the big picture.

Secondly, it will influence the career you choose.

There are advantages and disadvantages of each Personality – highlight those that apply to you:

'THE HIGH SKYDIVER'

Sees new ways of doing things
Finds creative solutions
Sees long term possibilities
Sees total picture - in 3D
Is unhurried. Doesn't worry too much
Sees links between subjects/topics
Thinks of many new alternatives
More 'Right side brain'
Enjoys free-flowing writing
Makes it up as he goes along
Takes risks happily
Enthuses others - supportive
Uses all resources together
Likes variety & excitement. New experiences
Skims through work very effectively
Doesn't always take the 'orthodox route'
Has a feel for a subject
Becomes totally involved in interesting topics
Tries new ideas/techniques.Likes trial & error
Likes open ended tasks
Sees the Big Picture

BUT:

Can forget important details
Delays, procrastinates before starting
Tends to work back from the answer
Doesn't like timetables
Only works in bursts
Forgets key resources (books)
Easily distracted
Doesn't file or rework notes
Not assertive - too easy going
Doesn't often plan in advance
Rushes into answers without thinking
Leaves worst until last - deals with only the aspects of a topic or subject that appeal
Tries to do too much at once
Doesn't work out priorities
Leaves things until the last minute
Can be very demanding
Hates detail
Doesn't check work
Tends to make guesses
Can be disorganised

'THE INTREPID EXPLORER'

Organises facts & materials well
Sees sequences in ideas
Enjoys problems and solutions
Approaches work in a structured way
Works things out well on paper
Works well on own
Is precise & thorough & meticulous
Plans everyday work & revision well
Sets clear goals & priorities
Reworks notes and essay plans
Can see how theory is applied
Isn't easily distracted
Organises time well: work and play
Reads instructions carefully
Researches exam syllabus thoroughly
Likes to understand every aspect of a topic
Likes to follow examples
Does what has to be done: gets on with it
More 'Left side brain' - 2D worker.
Works step by step. Sequence is important
Is good at finding information, using resources

BUT:

Needs too much data before starting work
Doesn't consult teachers/friends enough
Won't try new approaches. Uncreative
Dislikes risk - often too cautious
Becomes too involved in theory
Can be set in his/her ways
Not a good group worker
Doesn't like to share problems
Trusts only in logic
Can be impatient
Sees only one way of doing something
Often preoccupied with details
Not especially creative/imaginative
Poor at inventing questions
Doesn't work well with others
Task completion important - not quality
Doesn't like change
Does not see the big picture

I do not have the puzzle tif

Successful learning model

Environment
I have the right kit
I have the right atmosphere
I am feeling positive

Upward Spiral of Success

Task
Information

Input
I have 3 learning senses
Visual
Auditory
Physical
I can adapt to use my best channel

Onwards and Upwards

Motivation
I want to do that again
I want to do it better
I can apply it to other situations

Positive attitude
I can do it
I want to do it
I like doing it
I feel good
I'm fit
I have a purpose

Reward
I know that I've achieved
I was successful
I am praised
I feel great;
That was a really great experience

Doing the task
I have a learning strategy
I know my learning personality
I will link right and left brain
hemispheres to learn in a multi-
intelligence way

Reinforcement
I understand
I intend to remember
I know how I best remember
I have the experience
I can link to what I know already

Unsuccessful learning model

Environment
I don't like where I work
I don't have any kit
I'm feeling bad about working

Input
Information is coming in through
my weakest learning channel

Task
Information

Negative Attitude
I can't do this
This is irrelevant
I am unhappy
I am unfit
I am stressed

Doing the task
I don't know how to approach this
I am going to do this just one way
and it's boring
I don't have the correct resources

Result
I don't want to remember
I don't know what I've achieved
I don't have any strategies for
remembering

No reward
That was unsuccessful
I recieved no praise
That was a bad experience
I don't understand

Demotivation
I don't want to do that again
I became worse and worse
I feel I'm useless

**Downward
Spiral**

Brain Frame

the 1st leap of lightning learning

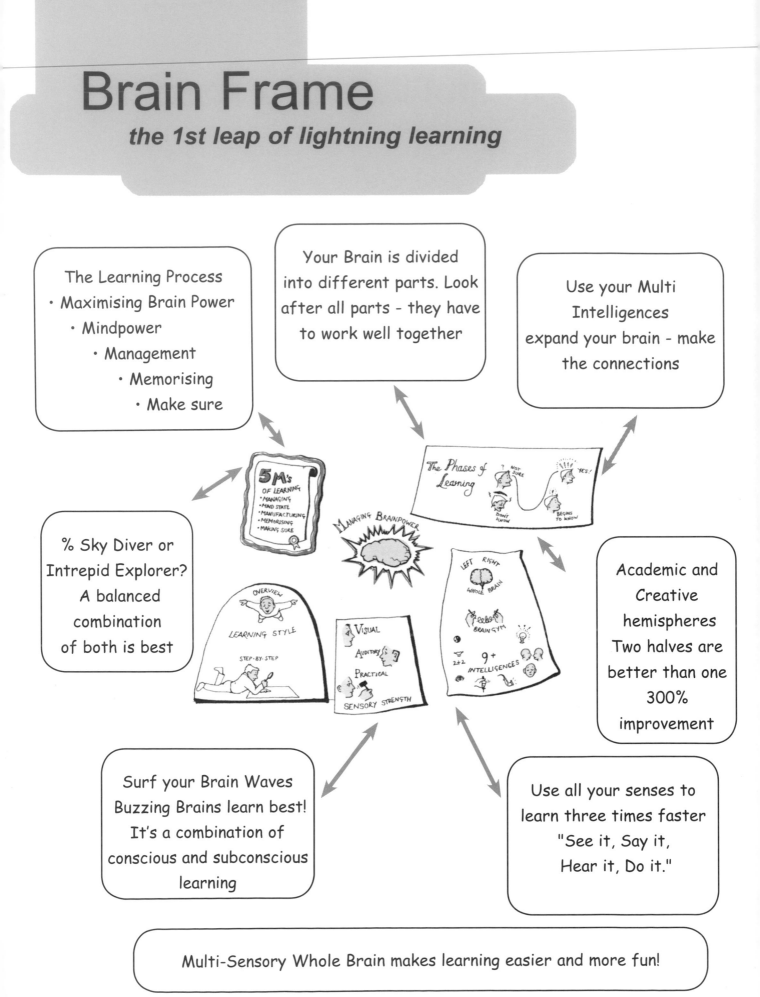

The Learning Process
- Maximising Brain Power
  - Mindpower
    - Management
      - Memorising
        - Make sure

Your Brain is divided into different parts. Look after all parts - they have to work well together

Use your Multi Intelligences expand your brain - make the connections

% Sky Diver or Intrepid Explorer? A balanced combination of both is best

Academic and Creative hemispheres Two halves are better than one 300% improvement

Surf your Brain Waves Buzzing Brains learn best! It's a combination of conscious and subconscious learning

Use all your senses to learn three times faster "See it, Say it, Hear it, Do it."

Multi-Sensory Whole Brain makes learning easier and more fun!

Mind State and Body State

Your mind is very powerful.

It has a tremendous influence on your feelings, emotions and your Middle Brain. If these feelings are negative, your middle brain will not be happy either and will filter out information reaching your Higher Thinking Brain and prevent learning.

The State of your mind is vitial to any success. It is about how you feel about yourself and what you believe. It is also about purpose, value, attitude and being able to change a negitative attitude to a positive one through the power of visualisation and imagination.

Your mind state is also affected by the state of your body - diet, fitness, hydration, sleep patterns and where you work. You can also exercise your brain to help link your hemispheres to make learning easier.

In section we will cover:

1. Self Belief and your Vision of Success

2. Attitude - Positive & Negative

3. Self Image

4. Imagination & Visualisation

5. Motivation

6. Managing Pressure

7. Setting Goals

8. Diet, Health & Fitness

9. Brain Exercises – opening your mind!

10. Juggling for your Genius

'You see things and say "why?"
I dream of things that never were, and I say "Why not?"'
George Bernard Shaw

Self Belief

What you believe about yourself is the single most important aspect of your education .

If you believe that you can succeed at doing something - you can, if you convince yourself you're going to fail you can fail.

Many of us in the past have thought we are 'bad' at a subject because we've been told so by others, or have come to believe it through initial failure. This is called a 'Learning Ceiling'.

If we set ourselves high standards, we can always improve. You can brake through your own learning ceiling.

For example, we often allow ourselves to fear the worst.

"I'm no good at Maths". You may have heard someone say that they thought you weren't very successful, another person may have reinforced that within earshot and soon enough you have a "learning ceiling" placed over you for Maths.

You can witness how it affects the greatest sports people, actors, musicians and inventors. Positive thoughts come from determination, ambition and having a:

Purpose and value

A very important factor in creating the right frame of mind is the ability to be able to discover a *reason* or *purpose* for your studies. Sometimes this is not obvious.

"Why am I studying algebra, no one uses algebra in everyday life?"

If you can discover *why* studying a particular subject or topic is or will be useful to you – it becomes *valuable* to you. And valuable things are worth keeping .

"I am studying alegra to pass GCSE in Maths: I need it to get a place in College to study Graphic Design which may lead to a career in special effects and work in TV or film production".

Learning algebra then becomes valuable to you. The brain prefers to learn things which are valuable and important to it. If you can't find a reason or purpose, you begin to give up – it doesn't seem valuable to you. Try to apply the subject or topic such as Essay Writing to a 'real life' situation. Ask why the subject is relevant or useful for your future.

Think of the bigger picture.
You'll find most, if not all topics will provide you with valuable life skills!

"I'm not sure why we are studying this?"

"What use will this be to me in the future?'

"Why is this important to me?"

"What's in it for me ?"

Remove the self-doubt and you will surprise yourself!

Have a Vision of The Future

To find a purpose and value in what you do, you need to have a Vision of the Future. This is about what you want to do with your life and what you want to be.

Just imagine yourself for a minute in ten or fifteen years time. What would you like to be doing ... *a brilliant sports-person, an actor, a wealthy businessman, an outstanding soldier, a fashion star, a doctor, engineer, lawyer ... who knows? You can't predict this, but you can dream and plan ahead.*

Day dreaming about the future is very important. It's also called **visualising** (see page 35 to learn how to do it) and it is all to do with the power of your multi-sensory imagination.

Day dreaming helps you see the **long term goal**. Then you can plan the steps that will help you get there.

And dreams and plans are good for you because they give you a purpose, a goal ... something to look forward to !

Creative and ambitious people visualise their success - golfers focus on thier swing and where the ball will land, Musicians often know the overall sound before they have created the detailed music, actors can 'walk through' their part without going near the stage, learners can visualise their success and their future in whatever they learn.

A US soldier imprisoned in Vietnam visualised and dreamt of his rounds of golf every day, shot by shot. When he was released he astounded everyone by hitting a perfect round. He wasn't surprised as he had perfected it in his mind - and had never once dreamt a bad round!

How to create a positive dream

1. Visualise the success

2. Imagine the person you want to be

3. Run a mental movie in your mind constantly

4. Only now start to consider what you could do to help yourself achieve your dream

5. Learn how to turn dreams into goals and then into action steps (See page 40)

Attitude - Positive versus Negative

Your attitude is about how you behave to others as well as to yourself.

Attitude affects altitude - how far you go in life.

Did you know that attitude is about behaviour and that your behaviour breeds good or bad behaviour in others? It is about the impression you give and your body language.

If you try to look more confident by walking with your head held high, people will think you are confident and that you can succeed.

If you try to look interested in a lesson, the teacher will think you are interested and will want to help you understand.

Attitude is very important to learning, Having a positive attitude helps you feel positive and this affects your Middle Brain which has so much to do with your state of mind and success.

A positive attitude helps brain cells connect more easily and learning improves.

Positive thinking is a lot more than blind faith. And its power over people's lives is awesome.

Optimists do better than pessimists in almost every aspect of life, often achieving more and enjoying greater success.

The pessimist believes bad events are a permanent condition. So, confronted by a setback, they often just give up. The optimist, however, attributes failure to temporary causes.
The optimist doesn't let one setback contaminate his whole life.

Positive People:

· See a difficult task as a challenge not a threat

· See opportunity not a problem

· Consider that all ideas and suggestions are possible

· Avoid "moaners"

· See setbacks as temporary

· Speak positively

· Enthusiastic communicators, positive gestures: smile
   often, cheerful tone of voice

· Present themselves well. Look forward not back.

For example - half way through your holiday do you say "Oh No, I've only got two weeks left" or "Great, I've still got two weeks left".

· Dream realistically - Positive thinkers learn how to visualise their "success" dream.
   'Success breeds success', as the saying goes.

· Create goals that are real possibilities.

· Break each task into small manageable chunks so success is constantly recognised.

Negative People:

Find fault

Look for problems

Expect the worst

Blame others

See a setback as permenent

Are tense and anxious

Feel hard done by

Compare themselves

Dislike positive statements

A positive attitude and personality are as important as good examination results.

Self-Image

It's about the ability and confidence to see yourself clearly as you want to be. *Being in control of this is a necessity - not an optional extra*

Low self esteem comes when you don't think you can live up to your own expectations or those of other people.

- Once you can 'see yourself' as others see you and when you can put yourself in other's shoes. Use your visual imagination to see how you want to be. Success will be much easier.

- You can improve your self-esteem and self-image by making a list of all your positive qualities and all those things you are good at as well as a list of your weaknesses and things you find difficult.

- Then look at what you have to do and a way to do it using your best qualities as well as your best learning channel and personality. Learn to know yourself better

- Change your negative reactions to positive ones - your behaviour will change and that's what gets results!

- Recognise you're unique - so don't fall into the trap of comparing yourself with others

- Believe you're worth it - admire yourself

- See all viewpoints

- Judge your real situation

- Be willing to change

BUILD YOUR SELF ESTEEM

Sometimes it is difficult to motivate yourself. We all lack confidence from time to time.

Think back and visualise an achievement.

1. My greatest success has been...

2. I am good at...

3. I have helped others by...

4. The best decision I ever made was...

5. If I am able to I want to ....

6. I believe I am good at ....

7. Something I have learnt recently to do is...

8. Something I am proud of is ....

9. My proudest moment has ....

10. The most difficult thing I ever did ....

Learn to imagine success and lock on to it like a guided missile

The Power of Imagination

Imagination is probably your most powerful thinking skill.

It is about using information or knowledge you already know and seeing it in another situation as well as inventing new ideas and creating images or pictures of them in your head.

Close your eyes and imagine what the world will be like in the year 2050. How do you imagine cars will look like. What sort of computers will we haveand how much of our lives will they control?

Imagination is excellent for CREATIVE THINKING. And creative thinking is one of the most important new skills of the 21st century.

Imagination is also linked to day dreaming, self esteem and being able to imagine your success and who you want to be.

We have already mentioned the US soldier and his ability to train his brain to play golf from a Vietnamese prison (see page 31)

Now consider these two tales:

A grandmother ran out of her house having heard a screeching of wheels and a loud thump and found her grandson trapped under a car. He was not seriuosly injured, but would become far worse if the car was not moved instantly. She summouned all her stength and mindpower - and lifted the car from her grandson, who scrambled to safety.

There was a football coach who carried out a survey of his players. He asked some to practise their penalties every day, and the second group to stop practising all together, and the third group to practise on the first and last days and imagine their 'penalty taking' success for 40 minutes each day. After two weeks the first group showed 20% improvement, the second group - showed 0% improvement.....and the third group - also made a 20% improvement!

So what would they have achieved if they had practised alot and used their imagination also to learn? Try this with your Revision.

So your mind is very powerful if you can imagine well.

Of course, a positive imagination is much better and it is approximately three times **FASTER AND BETTER!**

Imagination means using "thought pictures".

The Power of Visualisation

Visualisation is a process by which you can make a word, story or situation come alive in your head by experiencing it and living it with all your senses. You can see things in a different setting or give them a different meaning.

Sometimes you have to visualise a problem from a different angle. Be creative - look for other solutions.

If you can Visualise well, your brain will react as if you are really experiencing it - and you can dream your success in detail without having to dream of any failure!

Visualisation is being able to "see images and pictures" in your mind. Visual Learners and people with good visual intelligence should use this skill.

It is like having a photographic memory or being able to see an image of something you want to create. Using all your sense one by one, layer upon layer, you build your own mental movie.

Architects have good visualisation - they can see the building in their mind's eye before they start to design it.

Visualisation can be used for revising and learning facts. You literally close your eyes and "see" them written on the back of your eyelids - or see them on a blank wall in front of you.

Visualisation must involve all your senses.

TRY THIS **TEST YOUR VISUAL ABILITY.**

The Rain Storm...
Hear the tolling thunder
See the skies change – the clouds
Hear the heavy drops of rain
Feel them trickle down your neck
Taste the rain in your mouth
Feel the fresh atmosphere
Smell the clean air . . .
If you can do this - you're visualising!

Motivation

This is your 'Get Up and Go'

(making yourself work ... even when you don't want to!)

We all need "get up and go" ! If we don't feel like studying, but we know we have to, we often find excuses to do something else! We are often heard to say: "I just can't seem to make myself work!"

It's not easy - in fact motivation and the self-discipline that goes with it are greatly underestimated Life Skills. "Motivation " - it is one of the most elusive words to define!

Here are some typical words that try to decsribe it:

Goals Drive Behaviour Focus Purpose Desire Aims Target

Motivation is a POSITIVE FORCE that propels us towards achieving a Goal, Aim or Target

Poor motivation is often linked with low confidence, not feeling good about yourself, fear of failing and generally negative vibes!

There are many instances when we feel de-motivated ... others when we feel enthusiastic and very positive. Can you think of those occasions when you've been de-motivated - or really fired up? Did they have successful outcomes?

Motivation Check List:
Circle those that affect you

Are any of these 'de-motivators' familiar

Not understanding

Poor marks

No praise for your efforts

Feeling ignored

Low confidence

Negative criticism

Frustration with studies

Lack of appreciation

Slow or even no progress

Being Late

Are any of these motivators familiar?

Praise and reward from teachers

A plan has worked

Steady improvement

Setting targets and producing work

Good marks

Someone says "thanks"

Being recognised as a hard worker

Understanding your work

Finishing work on time

Feeling proud of your work

So How Do I Motivate Myself

Tips For Keeping Yourself Motivated

Re-assess your goals often. Record them in your Time Planner. Try to look into the future - if you're going to enjoy your future life, you've got to learn to work hard.

What do you want when you're grown up - constantly remind yourself.

Break your work down into **manageable 'bite-size' chunks:** it's less daunting.

Set yourself sensible time-limits, and rewards at the end of each session.

Plan your day - make sure the work is timetabled, and your play!

Be determined to do the work. (you can even pretend to be a martyr sometimes!)

Ask yourself "Why have I been set this? What's the purpose?"

Take a pride in presentation and performance. Develop a reward system for successes

Find someone to help you understand. Motivation requires plenty of individual recognition

Find someone who will praise your efforts.

Look back at other successes, such as high marks ...

and believe you can do it.

Develop a mental picture of yourself succeeding

Look after your health by eating, resting, exercising appropriately

Avoid comparisons with others

Set "SMART" Targets (See page 40)

Motivation and Attitude are therefore also vital factors in creating the right frame of mind for learning

WHAT DO YOU WANT? - try this self assessment	Yes	Sometimes	Never
I like working with others			
I want opportunities to care or give service to others			
I want to set goals and reach targets			
I want competition			
I want opportunities to learn and develop			
I want opportunities to be creative			
I want opportunities to solve problems/find solutions			
I want opportunities to find new things			
I know my reason/purpose for studying			
I want to prove I can do it myself			
I want to prove I can do it to my family and friends			
I want to go to university / college			
I want to have more free time			
I want to be in control of my future			
I want to catch up on what I missed out on			
I want to be motivated when times are difficult and slow			
I want to occupy my time positively			
I have always wanted to know how to study			
I like to learn new things			
I want a challenge			
I want to be more confident			
I want to improve my life skills			
I want career opportunities			

Managing Learning and Pressure

It's vital to create a happy frame of mind and for a settled frame of Mind you must have harmony between mind and body There is no doubt that any form of worry, anxiety or too much stress blocks your learning channels. It affects all parts to your brain

What is Pressure?

It is a build up of tension, anxiety and strain. It is a form of stress. Everyone experiences pressure. Without some stress we would have nothing to motivate, challenge or stimulate us. We all have Optimum Stress Levels (OSL). If we go above or below this level, significantly, we begin to "feel" the pressure.

Some can cope with stress easier than others. Failing to cope is not a sign of weakness.

Too little stress can be bad for you too. You can train yourself to be better at handling stress.

Physical symptoms:

Eating habits change (more/less) ● too little, too much sleep ● stomach disorders ● nervous habits, fidgeting etc. ● high blood pressure ● headaches, cramps, muscle spasms ● breathlessness ● crying ● smoking/drinking more ● clumsiness ● violence ● nausea ● "butterflies" ● sweaty palms

Psychological symptoms:

Low self confidence, self esteem ● guilty feelings ● phobias and obsessions ● loss of interest ● poor memory and concentration ● failing to finish tasks ● irritation and anger ● procrastination ● trivial tasks ● lonely, isolated ● hyperactive ● indecisive ● racing mind ● fearing the future.

So the Psychological and Physical state affects how your brain works.

What causes anxiety/tension?

There are any number of causes – and what stresses one person need
not stress another. Look at the list below and highlight any that you recognise:

Our expectation to achieve. Failure.	Change in schools/recreation.
Poor motivation. Over-motivation.	Too much success .
Multi-decisions.	Over-tired.
Insufficient free time.	Revision and exams.
Poor planning. Leaving things until the last minute.	Travel delays.
Work mounting up.	Moving home.
Failing to reach targets.	Peer group pressure. Bullying
Other people - (annoying/demanding.)	Illness - Poor fitness.
Being constantly late.	Trouble with family
Distractions. Interruptions. Noise.	Incompetence or imagined incompetence.
Failing to balance hopes and desires with the reality of life.	Loss of a friend

How to handle pressure

Here some clear and simple ways of controlling stress:

Constructive self-talk - Positive internal chat calms you down and helps motivation.

Increase your oxygen input – Your brain uses 60% of your intake of oxygen. Breathe deeply, hold it for a few seconds. Relax your shoulders and arms. Breathe out. Sit up straight, keep your spine straight and allow blood and oxygen to flow properly.

You'll begin to unwind.

Recognise that you're stressed – spot the danger signals. Resolve to deal with it.

Know what relaxes you and what you enjoy – what stimulates you.

Know when to stop – when to say "No".

Organise your time sensibly – balancing work and play. Timetable yourself carefully.

Plan your daily routine – set realistic targets.

Attend Yoga, meditation, relaxation or massage sessions.

Exercise – it allows your body to work off tension, increases oxygen/blood circulation and often gives your mind a break.

Eat sensibly – a good diet is very important (see page 42)

Plan in Rewards. Celebrate success. Small successes deserve rewards just as much as big successes!

Sleep well – relax before you go to sleep. Don't become over tired: don't cut down on your optimum sleep time.

Catch yourself doing it well – Self-praise. Talk positively to yourself. "I did that really well!"

Play relaxing music – it is amazing how this calms the mind.

Try to predict difficult times ahead - use a monthly calendar. Work out the "Pressure Points ".

If in doubt – seek help and advice. Often a problem shared is a problem solved!

Notes

Setting your own Targets and Goals

If you can discover the Purpose and value of your studies your motivation and attitude will improve. It is a method of creating and setting **performance standards.** It will help your behaviour change quickly and you will feel happier and more positive if you know what you have to do, by when and how you are going to do it.
You should consider your AIMS or OBJECTIVES. (These are your goals.)

Goal Setting

Goals - what you would like to achieve in 5 years

Targets - what you need to achieve in a term or year towards your goal

Tasks - what you need to do today and this week towards your targets

Setting Smart Targets

This requires some practice, and should be dealt with in some detail.

1. Take each area of your life. Work. Family. Sport/Fitness. Personal/Activities
2. Write down 5 things you would like to improve in each area over the next 12 months.
3. Make them:

S   Specific so they can be visualised

M   Measurable so you can always have a benchmark

A   Attainable. With a reason or a purpose in mind, you

will need to check you are able to succeed

R   Realistic - not beyond reasonable. Be sure your goals all 'pull in the

same direction'

T   Timed. They should be tied to a timescale. Sometimes you may have to

break down your tasks into chunks

To set a Goal - for example: " I want to juggle three balls".

Steps / Action	By When (Timescale)
1. Make sure the basic throw is correct X 200	End of Day 2
2. Practise with two balls to make sure timing and 'flight path' are correct. Catch both. X 200	End of Day 4
3. Practise with three balls - only throwing, no catching X 200	End of day 5
4. Practise throwing and catching all three - as many times as possible in a minute X 200	End of week

Setting goals is a vital process for your success - imagine your targets.

Ask: " What's in it for me?" TAKE CHARGE OF YOUR DESTINY.

Below is a visual example of planning Course Work.

Diet, Fitness and Sleep

You will not learn successfully if you are tired, stressed, unfit, dehydrated and have not nourished your brain.

Feeding the Brain. Brains need stomachs!

Fish - particularly fatty fishes such as mackrel, salmon and sardines

Fruit - particularly kiwi fruit and bananas which plenty of Vitamin C that helps oxygenate the blood, repairs cells and are a good supply of potassium

Green Vegetables - rich in B vitamins which help memory

High energy Carbohydrates such as pasta and oats.

Draining the Brain

Coffee, alcohol, high sugar and processed foods, satuarated fats

A diet of processed snacks such as crisps, chips and sweets will cause tiredness and depression as well as slow down your learning

Do not skip meals especially breakfast, the brain uses two thirds of the body's total intake of glucose and needs a steady supply. All research suggests that to deprive your body of nutrients and essential vitamins or to eat food that is inappropriate will lead each time to a slow, laborious brain response. This means that, over a period of time, you will learn slower than otherwise. Those who ate a bowl of cereal for breakfast before an exam did better than those who did not.

Water - go with the flow - drink H_2O

Pure water is vital for the brain. Drink plenty of clear water - water is conductor of electricity and your brain functions with electrical impulses – a headache can often be caused by de-hydration too. Drink a minimum of 1 litre each day; it heightens energy, improves concentration and helps your learning. If you exercise and sweat alot, drink up to 2/2.5 litres to replace it. Avoid to many sugery drinks, they are counter-productive.

Fitness - Exercising your Brain

Your brain uses up to 60% of your oxygen supply.
Playing sport, walking, swimming or any other
aerobic exercise will not only make your body fitter
but your brain as well.
Movement plays an essential part in learning. It
activates the network of brain cells.
It increases the flow of blood to the brain
It develops the number of connections between brain cells
It promotes connections between the right and left hemispheres
It encodes new learning in the motor memory
It integrates mind and body.
If you don't exercise much, less oxygen gets to the brain and
the less effective it is.

You will also be affected by:

Where you work

Managing your Time

Planning

Having a 'Learning Supporter

We deal with this in the 4th Leap
on page 61

Sleep and Your Brain

Your brain needs to rest - but for about 20% of your sleep time
you are in a Theta brain wave state when you dream. This is
known as REM Time (Rapid Eye Movement Time) and happens
2-4 times a night and can vary. Sleep deprivation, therefore, can
be extremely harmful to learning. Dreaming is process of 're-filing
or housekeeping'; it is a process of reflection and puzzling out
problems. The rest of your sleep time you are in a Delta brain wave
state (deep sleep). We need a total of 8 hours sleep to be fully fit.
Researchers agree that sleeping helps consolidate memories.
We can help our brain work things out and re - inforce memory by
creating an "Alpha brain wave state" just before you go to sleep.
Look back at page 15 to help you do this.

Water is Important Because:

It transports nutrients all over the body.
It aids in digestion and converting carbohydrates to energy.
Even a little dehydration causes slower thinking.
Your body will run more smoothly".
Your body – blood, muscles, oxygen & bones all require adequate
water to work efficiently.

Brain Link

BRAIN EXERCISES – *open your mind* Link the hemispheres - energise the brain

There are exercises which make your Brain much more receptive to learning, because physical movement stimulates brain function and it helps link both hemispheres. You will feel more relaxed and your negative feelings will drift away – and, because stress blocks your Learning Channels, these exercises are especially important.

To put yourself in the right mind state - to help you achieve all the areas we have covered in this section you should try:

Being Ambidextrous (using both hands to equal strength)

Marching using opposite legs and arms
Drawing 'infinity' signs with both hands at the same time, moving in opposite directions. Writing your name in mirror image with both hands at the same time. Learn to juggle (see page 45).

Oxygenate the brain

Put your thumb and index under your collar bone and massage the hollows. It increases blood flow to the brain.

Adjust your electrical pathways

Put one hand just below your belly button and the thumb and index finger of your other hand on your above and below your lips. Rub gently side to side. Your brain alone produces enough electricity to light up at least two 60 watt lights and this exercises helps bring the electrical balance back into your whole body.

Open up your brain network.

Put one ankle over the other knee; cross your hands in your lap. Rest your tongue on the roof of your mouth and breath slowly. At the same think of subject and let all you know about that subject flood back into your mind. This is an excellent exercise to do before a lesson or revision session. It helps you remember what you already know.

Switch off the Panic - great in exams

Above your eyebrow are two neuro-vascualar points. When you panic blood rushes away from Your Thinking Brain. But if you massage these two points gently it will help the blood return and helps you concentrate again.

The Art of Juggling for Genius

1. One Ball
Juggling

Throw the ball from one hand to the other.

Relax. Stand with your legs slightly apart, with

weight on your heels.

Try to throw the ball from just above your waist.

Aim for a point about 10cm above your head

Now let the ball drop. Say "Throw" and "Drop".

2. The Throw up!

As you begin to throw the ball push up

your arm, then hand and finally spring the ball

from your fingers.

Focus on where the ball will begin to drop.

3. Throwing & Catching - It's good *throwing* that

counts. Concentrate on throwing rather than

catching. We tend to catch by instinct -

don't worry. It takes care of itself.

Watch the ball until just after it reaches the

top of its flight. Now close your eyes.

Catch at waist height. You'll be surprised

how you'll still catch it... or try throwing

clapping and then catching to ensure height.

4. Throwing Two Balls and dropping both

Place 2 balls in each hand. Throw with your

stronger hand. Just after it begins to drop from

the top of its flight, throw the second ball

Don't try to catch them. Let them drop.

They should land close to your feet.

Watch the ball's path and flight.

This is vital for later.

5. Throwing Two Balls and catching one

Now try catching one only.

Say "Throw, Throw"

Check your flight path and balance.

6. Throwing Two Balls and catching both

As above.. If you have to stretch to catch it, let it drop.

Try again. Check your stance,

posture, throw, balance...and your self-belief!

7. Throwing Three balls - let them all drop

Place 2 Balls in your strongest hand, one in the other.

Start with the two ball hand.

Throw Ball One (say "One") - as it begins to drop from its

height, throw Ball Two (say "Two") - and when it begins to

drop, throw Ball Three (say "Three").

Throw all three, allow your weaker hand to

catch Ball One only.

Now practise throwing with 2 Balls in your

weaker hand. Always start with the two ball hand.

8. Throw three and catch two

Throw all three

Catch "Ball one" as before.

Catch "Ball Two".

Ignore "Ball Three"....but watch its flight path.

9. Throw three and catch three (The Cascade)

Throw as above. Catch them only if they are in easy reach

of your hands. Don't expect it to be perfect first time: you may

become worse before you get better.

10. The Infinity 3 ball Cascade

If you have achieved a single juggle

....WELL DONE!

Now you need to keep it going!

To continue after you've thrown "Ball 3"

think of the next ball as "Ball 1" again... not "Ball 4!"

This time you will throw the fourth 'ball' from your weaker

hand. Try saying "throw, throw, throw" to help the rhythm.

Visualise yourself succeeding. Relax, slow down by throwing

the ball a little higher. You've done it!

Brain Frame

the 2nd leap of lightning learning

Positive people improve performance
Negative nigglers get nowhere
Attitude determines your Altitude

Have a Vision of the Future
Day dreaming is good for long term goals
Set SMART Targets

Motivation propels us towards a change in behaviour.

Get up and Get on

If you believe you can, you can.
If you think you can't, you can't.
"Success comes in cans, not cannots"

Brain Exercises to link the hemispheres and increase connections.

Juggling for Genius

You need a Purpose and Value
"What is in it for you"

Spot Symptoms of Pressure - manage worry

Power of Visualisation
Seeing pictures in your Mind

Power of Imagination
Think like a Genius

Feed your Brain, feed your body
Foods for Thoughts!

Self Image
How you see yourself and how others see you

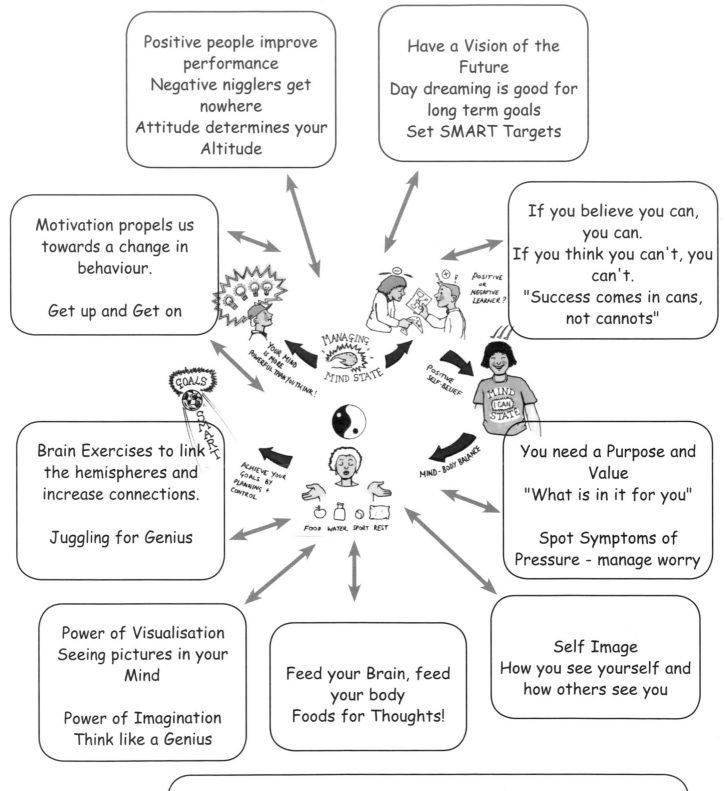

Your Mind State and Body State greatly affects Learning

Multi-Sensory Intelligences and Thinking Skills

Intelligence is sometimes called "ways of knowing or doing". It is about making as many brain connections as possible by doing and thinking in different ways.

In Leap One, you learnt that every time you had a thought or experience your brain made connections. This chapter deals with "IQ" and "EQ" - Intellectual and Emotional Intelligence You have many different Intelligences and these can be used to help you think in different ways.

Thinking increases your Intelligence - using your **Multi Intelligences** develops your **Thinking Skills.**

In section we will cover:

1. Thinking Skills - General skills
2. Logical & Lateral
3. Intelligence and Multi Sensory Learning Skills
4. Examples of Multi Intelligence Studying
5. Creative Thinking
6. Bottom Line, Over & Non Thinking
7. Drawing on your Brain Power

Notes

Thinking Skills

THINKING SKILLS AND MULTI INTELLIGENCES

Thinking skills are about the different ways you use your brain to sort out information and turn it into knowledge and meaning. It is about how you use knowledge and information in different situations and contexts and how you communicate it to others.

Being able to 'think' in different ways is one of the most important skills of the 21st century. This is because the world is changing so fast that much of what you learn today will soon be out of date and you will always be having to find new solutions and learn new skills.

There are many different ways to think.

These include :

putting knowledge into a sequence of importance - ***prioritising***

seeing similarities in different information - ***sorting and classifying***

seeing what is important about the information - ***evaluating***

using the knowledge in different situations - ***transferring***

spotting a pattern emerging from the information - ***analysing***

guessing outcomes from situations - ***predicting***

using the information in an ordered way - ***planning***

seeing new uses for knowledge - ***creating solutions***

finding answers using information - ***problem solving***

explaining information to others - ***communicating***

proving that information is correct - ***testing solutions, hypothesising***

seeing what is good and bad about a situation - ***criticising***

There are also different Thinking Personalities.

We discussed these in the last section when talking about Mind Power and your brain.

Lateral and Creative Thinkers:

Tend to be more right hemisphere dominant

Tend to be Sky Divers

Find new solutions to problems

Link up thoughts in a random order

Come up with some "whacky" ideas

Are good at brainstorming

Linear and Logical Thinkers:

Tend to be more left hemisphere dominant

Focus on the obvious solutions

Link up thoughts in a logical, sequential way

Use judgement and sense to select ideas

> *A cowboy road into town on Friday.*
>
> *He stayed two nights and left on Monday,*
>
> *How is this possible? Solution below*
>
> *This is a form of lateral or 'sideways' thinking. It's very good for you and makes you use your Right brain and not just your Left one!*
>
> *It's a whole brain skill!*
>
> Answer - His horse is called Friday

Positive Thinkers:

Find a purpose in what they have to do

Believe that they will succeed or at least try their best

See problems as challenges

Keep an open mind

Use positive language

Have a positive attitude and body language

Are good to be with

Negative Thinkers:

Look at everything as a chore or waste of time

Don't believe they will succeed even before trying

Make excuses and blame other people

Give up easily

Look fed up

Moan, complain and criticise

Are not good to be with

> *Which Characteristics seem to match you most?*

Using your Multi Intelligences helps you learn in a Multi Sensory Way and develops your Thinking skills. You will enjoy learning and remember more.

Your many intelligences

LINGUISTIC

This is the skill you use when talking or writing

Typical characteristics are:

Keen on reading (literature), verse and writing

Learning well from listening. Enjoys conversation, wide vocabulary and a confident command of language -

Explaining or instructing with ease

Taking notes, writing letters, communicating comfortably through words

Focusing on word games - on TV or in newspapers

Enjoying discussion or argument

Putting information into own words with ease

It's a vital intelligence, because language is the essence of communication – you will always need to express your thoughts or feelings. Expanding your own vocabulary is therefore especially important - so try using a Thesaurus.

Language – the essential communication channel

MATHEMATICAL/LOGICAL

This is the skill you use with numbers, sequencing, logical thought and under-standing 'systems'.

Typical characteristics are:

Working step by step, putting into sequences. Prefering order and making logical explanations.

Enjoying numbers, puzzles and problem solving more scientific topics.

Quick with mental arithmetic. Calculating totals, scores, percentages, bets!

Good at planning ahead - time - diary!

Takes a systematic approach.

Quick at recognising of links between things.

Enjoying working things out. Analysis.

Estimating quantity / amounts with ease.

You can be very logical and systematic without being a maths genius. For instance planning a journey from A to B will require logical prior planning and preparation for every step of the way and in every area of the journey.

It's about what's important - and in what order

NB The first two intelligences are the dominant ones in schools - they are very 'left hemisphere' friendly....that's fine is you've a strong left brain as you'll have found studying easier - but if you're a physical / practical learner you may have found it more difficult....read on because everyone can benefit from using all intelligences

PHYSICAL / PRACTICAL

This is the skill you use when you handle, build or move. It is a 'constructive' intelligence, it is physically active (running, sports, dancing) and involves co-ordination and motor skills. Many people see themselves as practical or 'hands on' personalities. This has been regarded as an inferior intelligence by some. It is an equally high intelligence.

Typical characteristics are:–

Enjoying making something - being 'involved'. DIY – a practical experience! Learning through 'concrete' materials.

Creating by doing – cooking, modelling and similar hobbies.

Enjoying practical games – jigsaws, lego.

Enjoying physical exercise - moving and doing.

Being tactile.

Experiencing through role play

Putting theory into practice.

The best learners learn ACTIVELY.

VISUAL/SPATIAL

This is the skill you use when you can 'picture' and imagine in your mind. It's an awareness of how things look, their size and shape. It's a 3D intelligence.

Typical characteristics are:-

Ease with design, drawing and building – diagrams, charts, videos, slides.

Estimating direction, navigation, maps and estimating distance

An awareness of space and position

Being able to visualise connections and links.

Planning layout. Being good at graphic design skills.

Being observant, having a 'photographic' ability in your mind.

Ease with pattern, shape and colour; mind maps, spidergrams, flow charts and explanatory diagrams.

Good at cycling, driving, manipulating remote control cars

Typically, most architects, designers, artists and photographers 'see' this as their dominant intelligence.

Visual ability also means seeing things from different angles: Which of these is longer - A or B ?

A   B   *What does the eye tell the brain ?*

Your answer: A: B: Same:

The answer is at the bottom of the page.

You made an assumption based on what you see - were you right?

See with your mind's eye.

Answer - b is slightly longer

MUSICAL

This is the skill we use daily – whether 'musical' by training or not. It's the ability to create, enjoy or sing along with music and to create rhythm or memorise a rhyme. Often it's subconscious – like foot tapping!

Typical characteristics are:

Listening to music Singing, humming, whistling.

Relaxing to music.

Playing the music in your mind - often catchy numbers.

Enjoying rhythm and beat.

Having a sense of melody

Being good at remembering verses, slogans, mnemonics – T.V. ads.are especially typical!

Remembering tunes and lyrics – associating events.

Learning by chanting

For many this is a greatly underestimated intelligence, sometimes not even recognised as such.

Why not turn this to your advantage when learning something really boring. You have the power to make it more interesting with music.

MUSICAL The power of popular music, T.V. advertisment jingles or radio commercials is immense – we often remember them even when we don't like them.

INTERPERSONAL

This is the skill you use daily to communicate and form a rapport with others. It involves the skill of speaking or writing in a way that others understand. It is an intelligence that considers other people's feelings.

Poor interpersonal skills can prove very damaging.

Typical characteristics are:

Being interested in others. Aware of moods.

Being sympathetic to feelings/ reactions. A good listener – 'the shoulder to cry on'

Being capable of reassuring and explaining. Informal chats are easy.

Being good at and enjoying solving problems/difficulties involving others.

A feeling of 'community' or 'teamwork'.

Willing to share ideas

Enjoy teaching/training/helping others understand.

This is such an important intelligence if you want to succeed as part of a group. If you feel 'OK' and can help others feel 'OK' then everyone will benefit ... and this is very true when you are learning!

Hear with your mind's ear!

INTRAPERSONAL

This is the skill you use within you. It's the 'Self Talk' referred to earlier – the skill to analyse and consider your own feelings and attitudes, successes and set - backs.

Typical characteristics are:

Understanding your own feelings, attitudes – private, independent thought.

Having determination and resolve.

Accepting change.

Analysing and correcting weaknesses.

Pondering on problems objectively.

Thinking positively.

Motivating yourself.

Having the ability to create an inner interest.

Having an ease at planning goals/ ambitions

Dreaming of success and making it reality.

Predicting the tough times.

Recording life in diaries.

Discovering purpose and relevance in learning.

*This is, therefore, your **Personal Intelligence**. It's essential for your **Motivation and Attitude**. We need it in all forms of learning and for all our lives!*

Success comes from within

INTUITIVE

This is the skill you possess to receive or perceive information that is not readily available to our five senses. It is often regarded as the most creative or highest form of intelligence.

Typical characteristics are:

The truth is in there!

The ability to solve a problem in a seemingly irrational and illogical way.

A sub-conscious analysis of a problem or situation.

"It came to me in a flash" solution finder.

Belief in a "6th sense".

Knowing something is right/wrong – but not being sure why.

Confidence to act on gut feelings

*It would be easy to disregard this **innate intelligence** as 'irrational behaviour' or guesswork. It's more than that - it comes from the power of the mind, the sophistication of the brain ... and it's very nature appears inexplicable.*

As we discover more and more about the ability of the mind, Intuitive Intelligence will become more understandable.

Your Intuitive Intelligence is working all the time – even when you're asleep!! It certainly helps with your work, learning and life in general.

Multi Intelligence assessment

Look back over each of the 8 Intelligences.

Consider which are your stronger and your preferred ones. Place them in order of :

A. Dominance	B. Preferred	Rank 1 (top) to 8
A	B	

1

2

3

4

5

6

7

8

9

10

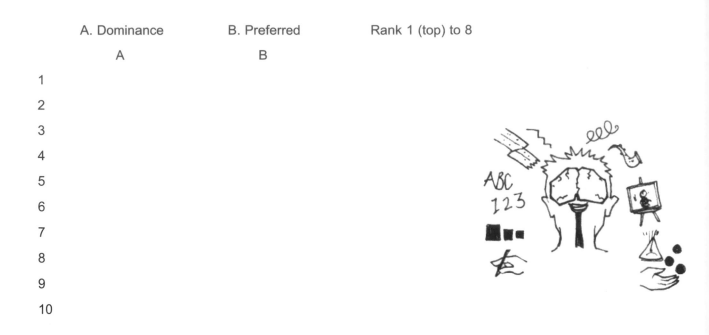

You can use different Intelligencies to do the same task.

Example:

"Illustrate the events leading up to the Second World War"

You could:-

1. Write an essay (Linguistic intelligence)

2. Give a talk (Lingistic / Interpersonal)

3. Turn it into a play or role play (Lingistic / Interpersonal)

4. Draw a diagram or Brain Frame. (Logical / Spacial)

5. Write a poem / sing or rap. (Linguistic / Musical)

6. Make up a game. (Logical / Physical)

Ask yourself which way would you like to learn and remember the best? You should try all of these.

You can compile your information from different sources using all your intelligences.

Books

Videos

Talking with others

Museums

and many more RESOURCES.

Make your learning multi-sensory, global and interesting – and you will increase your thinking and remembering skills!

We look at this in the fifth leap.

Using Multi-Sensory Intelligences.

If you're studying a topic, create your combination from this list:-

1. Rephrase question/topic heading/problem – Create a (new) question (Linguistic)

2. Seek a logical path through the topic. Break into 'bite size' chunks. Flow chart. (Mathematical / logical)

3. Highlight main points / facts / headings. (Physical / practical)

4. Talk your way through the task (Intrapersonal)

5. Make a brain frame/ as you go (main point / fact only) use colours. (Visual / spatial)

6. Visualise in your mind's eye. (Visual / spatial)

7. Draw a Diagram / cartoon / charts / model? (Spatial)

8. Listen to non lyrical music. Create mnemonics, rhymes, rhythms. (Musical)

9. Speak difficult parts out aloud. (Musical)

10. Tape record key ideas / facts. (Musical)

11. Plan your time: 35-40 mins max. then break. (Mathematical / logical)

12. Tick each heading / sub heading as you complete it / understand it. (Physical / practical)

13. Keep some movement going. (Physical / practical)

14. Talk positively to yourself – keep yourself going. (Intrapersonal)

15. Build in rewards. Praise yourself. (Intrapersonal)

16. Discuss with others, swop notes. (Interpersonal)

17. Build in brief 'review time' – what have I achieved? (Intrapersonal)

18. Summarise topic in as few words as possible - make sure it is 'full enough' to make sense. (Linguistical)

"It ain't what you do, it's the way that you do it . . . That's what gets results!"

Example – Multi-Sensory Work Session

Notes/Task:
Describe a subject or topic where you could use all of the above methods

---

Creative Thinking:

Creative Thought is the product of Right and Left Hemisphere, Skills, Mind and Body Harmony and a sense of positive purpose.

This another one of the most important skills of the 21st Century - Creative thinkers do not always look for the obvious. They are often the' inventors of tomorrow '.

Creative thinking happens best when we are not trying too hard.

Often we consciously focus too hard and block creativity by allowing the Reptilian Brain to take control. We worry - and this is harmful and unproductive. Vary work and conditions - allow your mind to freewheel! This is when Flashes of Inspiration and periods of Creative Flow are likely.

What people misunderstand about Creativity

· "Only intelligent, "arty", scatty people are creative. It's rare and difficult. It hurts!"

· "Only the young are creative"

· Creativity is expensive on time

Some ideas for stimulating Creative thoughts

- Enjoy Activities and Pastimes - gain general experience

- Plan in "Creative Time"

- Set goals and targets realistically

- Talk to others, discuss ideas, develop interpersonal skills

- Create visual notes (Brain Frames, Mind Maps) and link ideas

- Learn to Brainstorm and link ideas

- Challenge deep rooted beliefs - "we are intelligent only of we pass exams".

- Reverse logic / reverse a situation (This is how disposable cameras were discovered)

- Be positive; negative thinking will restrict your creative imagination

- Never "bin" an idea; it could prove useful

- Focus on inspiration - Brainstorm ideas - Relaxation - Control your pressure

- Ignore logical "structure" - don't follow only obvious solutions

- Expect to find new approaches/ideas - keep an open mind

As you come up with ideas, ask yourself:

· Can / should I alter this?

· How else can I use this idea?

· Could I work smarter, more efficient, faster?

· Can these ideas be used together / combined?

· Has this been done before?

How many uses can you think of for a piece of blu tac? How many can you think of in a minute?

Intuitive Thinking

Intuition is an insight into a person, situation or place that proves accurate but without any reason. It is not fully understood - it is rarely recommended and yet seems to be a baseline skill for historical "genius".

We all have gut-feelings, hunches about things or without knowing why we can sense that something is right or wrong.

Intuitive thinking is your mind's way of saying *'beware' or 'go for it'*

1. Listen to what it is telling you. Do you have a good or bad feeling?

2. You should discuss it with a close friend or colleague. What's their opinion?

3. Test it against logical or Bottom Line Thinking (see over the page.)

4. Record everything that comes into your mind - don't analyse it

Sometimes when we do focus on "believing something will happen" actually makes it happen.

We term this a "Self Fulfilling Prophecy".

This is when you believe something will happen, so strongly that you:

* Show it in your body language, face, movement, appearance

* Talk as though it's a foregone conclusion

So, when you say to yourself "I'm going to fail the driving test" you subconsciously indicate it to everyone.

When you fail, both you and others say "Oh well. I'm not surprised. I told you so!" What's the antidote to this?

Positive Thinking and Constructive Self Talk and a Positive Attitude

"Bottom Line Thinking"

Bottom-line thinking involves making a realistic assessment of the worst possible situation by analysis of all the possible consequences.

Pick the worst situation. Could you handle it?

Can you estimate how to avoid it? What's the "bottom line"?

It reasssures us and often removes stress.

It has many benefits:

· It provides a realistic view of a situation.

· It puts things into perspective

· It prepares us for pressure

· It allows us to plan ahead

· We can estimate a variety of solutions

· It helps control potential anxiety

And we tend to avoid the Bottom Line

situation as a result!· We are less "negative".

We use it when we have a:

· deadline

· test

· decision

· challenge

· problem

When we are:

Worried

Tired

Potentially out of control

Feeling negative

Over Thinking

This is when we worry about something or focus on a task / problem to the exclusion of all other matters. It can be very dangerous, both to health and confidence.

We often fall into this trap when we fear failure - when we have not discussed it with anyone and when we need to blame others! We imagine the worst, can't find a sensible explanation and misunderstand. We can't see the wood for the trees! We operate poorly. We lose sleep, upset others and often panic.

Solutions

· Put distance between you and the problem

· Analyse the cause

· Share it with others

· Apply positive and Bottomline skills

· Apply relaxation skills to encourage:

Non Thinking Skills

This is best described as a relaxed yet focused state of mind. It's necessary as air food and water! It's a mindless task of physical exertion, it's Alpha brain wave music, meditation, planned relaxation and fun daydreaming

Benefits

· You switch off

· Your Brain is off even if the lights are still on!

· You can reflect, analyse and "re-frame" your thoughts·

Drawing on your Brain Power

We can learn to help our Right Brain become better involved by drawing

To be able to doodle or sketch is very useful in the learning process - but it can also 'free up' our two hemispheres and help them work together.

Look at the drawing below, use a pencil and a clear piece of paper :

- Draw this with your usual hand but keep the image upside down

- Find an undisturbed place. Listen to music that is about 60 beats a minute (in line with your heartbeat)

- Concentrate on the lines and shapes not on the logical picture of the girl.

- Start either from the top and work down, or the bottom and work up.

- Don't be afraid to rub out mistakes.Take plenty of time.

- As you draw, ignore the meaning of the pictures, focus on the overall view upside down.

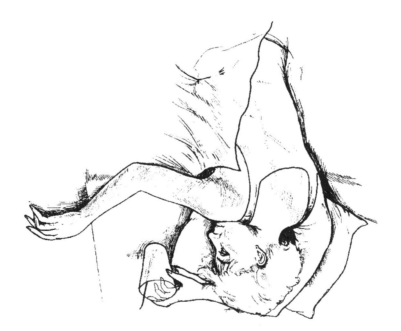

After you have copied everything down, turn over the paper. You should find that your picture is more accurate that you expected. If this is the case, it is because your Right hemisphere was allowed to play a full part. The left hemisphere didn't interfere.

This sort of exercise is great for switching on creativity and imagination.

You should also have enjoyed this in a relaxed state of mind - so Mind and Brain should be fine. Your brain is more prepared to tackle any problem now!

If you're feeling really brave, try the same exercise again - but with your other hand!

Remember - your left hemisphere controls the right side of your body, the right hemisphere controls the left.

Like juggling, this helps you link your brains!

Brain Frame
the 3rd leap of lightning learning

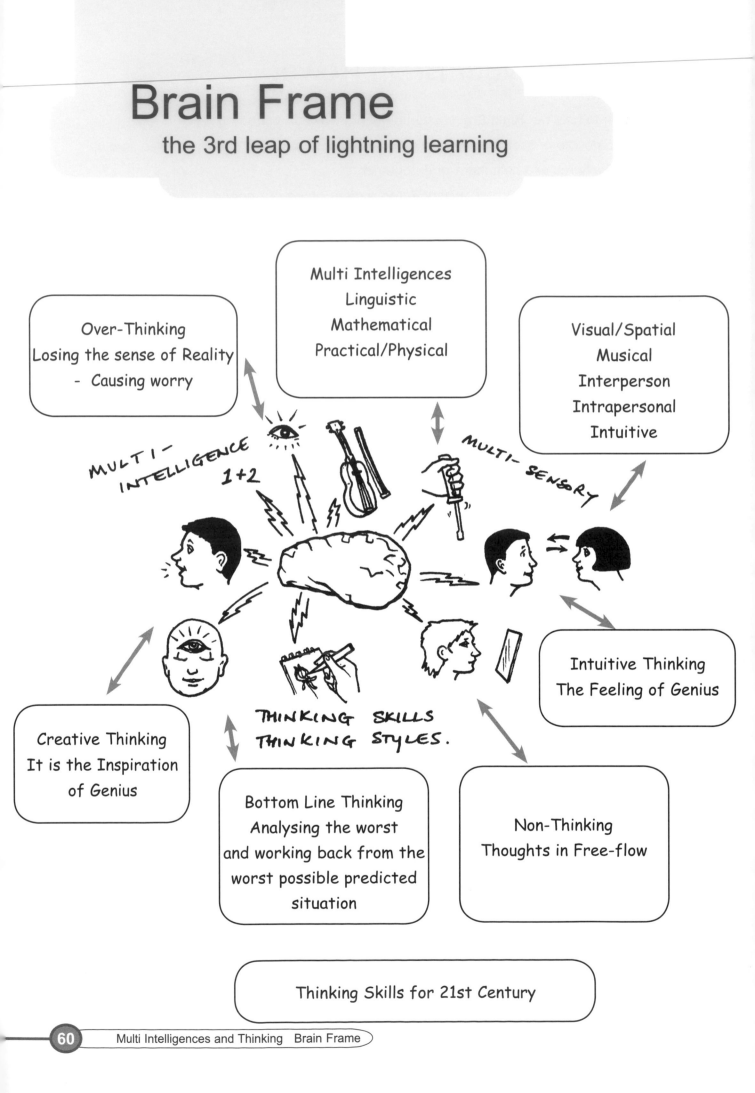

Over-Thinking
Losing the sense of Reality
- Causing worry

Multi Intelligences
Linguistic
Mathematical
Practical/Physical

Visual/Spatial
Musical
Interperson
Intrapersonal
Intuitive

MULTI-
INTELLIGENCE
1+2

MULTI-SENSORY

THINKING SKILLS
THINKING STYLES.

Intuitive Thinking
The Feeling of Genius

Creative Thinking
It is the Inspiration
of Genius

Bottom Line Thinking
Analysing the worst
and working back from the
worst possible predicted
situation

Non-Thinking
Thoughts in Free-flow

Thinking Skills for 21st Century

The Fourth Leap into Lightning Learning

Planning and Organisation

Prior planning and preparation prevents poor performances

Being in control of your life is essential. This requires you to organise and plan

what you do

how you do it and

when you do it.

Greater control over you life means more free time, a happier life and greater chance of

success. So use this chapter to give yourself more freedom

In section we will cover:

1. Why is planning and organisation important?

2. Your Learning Environment

3. The 'Kit'

4. The Ideal Study Session

5. Planning your Time

Notes

Why Plan?

Why is planning and organisation important?

So far you will have a good idea of the way you work best. You will be able to choose the ideal learning channels and multi sensory intelligences you need for a variety of topics.

You will be able to control your state of mind and motivation to work in the most positive of ways.

The important point to realise is that many students underachieve, despite being in control of their individual learning strengths because they fail to take into account their daily, weekly and monthly organisation.

You shouldn't have any trouble ... should you ?

But many people do have trouble planning and organising to study.......

Do you know why?

Think about it!

What's your answer?

Answer it now. Don't delay

Don't put it off.

Answer now ... not tomorrow

it's **PROCRASTINATION. . . . .**

"Procrastination is the thief of time!" and is the ability we have to put things off until tomorrow . . . until the last minute.

Making excuses

How do you explain why you're not working?

Perhaps you use some of these well known "pupil – quotes":

"I just can't seem to concentrate"

"I've lost my books."

"The deadline isn't for ages"

"The dog ate my homework assignment"

"I'll just get a drink."

"Dad, tell me again about when you played that wonderful game as centre-forward."

"I can revise outside!"

"I work better late at night, after my favourite programmes."

"No problem ... I'll get up early and do it."

"I've just remembered ... I have to 'phone..."

"I promised to do the washing up!"

"I've run out of time!"

I bet you've tried some or all of these ....   but who's fooling who?

Your Learning Equipment and Environment

So ... eventually you decide to work:

You approach your work area ... and what do you need ?

Answer these questions: tick the boxes

The Place: The Kit!

EQUIPMENT CHECKLIST   *Tick*

Pens, pencils, rulers, colours, highlighters	
Plastic wallets	
Paper - all types	
Index cards	
Timetables and planners	
Calculator	
Ink & Cartridges. Corrector pen	
Paper clips	
Rubber, corrector white-out	
Tapes. Discs Books Dividers, files, hole punchers	

ENVIRONMENT

The conditions in which you work also affect your state of mind.

It's important you know:

■ The room in which you work should be comfortable, airy, well lit, well equipped and organised.

■ Some like background, non-lyrical music; others absolute silence.

■ Some like tidy desks, others like a structured spread of information on one desk.

■ Some like to work totally alone; others in small groups; and others with teachers.

These are environmental factors, and you should begin to work out which suits you best. It'll help your frame of mind and make you more positive and confident.

THE PLACE YOU NEED:

☐ A bed to study on
☐ Good room temperature
☐ Lots of light
☐ Loud wordy music, plus T.V
☐ A roaring log fire (in winter of course!)
☐ A really soft, comfy armchair
☐ Loads of interruptions from friends
☐ All the books easily within reach
☐ A good table and chair that match in height
☐ Chatty friends
☐ Water
☐ Posters
☐ The correct texts and notes
☐ Telephone
☐ Pens, pencils, boxes, folders etc.
☐ Computer CD ROM Internet

The Ideal Work Session

The best work sessions should comprise of some or all of the following suggestions:

Prior Planning

Consider what you want to study.

Check it is the right topic to be concentrating on at this stage; check timetable.

Plan to work for 30-40 minutes.

Break your topic up into manageable chunks - no more than seven main headings.

Try to split each main heading into no more than seven 'bite size' parts.

Plan in Overview Time - what does the topic involve, how much do I know already? Allocate time to your topic main headings.

Work area

Quiet, perhaps with non lyrical music depending on what you're revising.

Light, both natural and general. A spot lamp will help, but not on it's own.

Make sure both chair and desk match.

Have all equipment ready - especially your notes, questions and past papers.

Put your plan on the wall along side your timetable and syllabus.

Brain Motivation

Intend to work! Find your purpose. Consider your Vision of Success.

Drink your water and do some brain exercises to link both hemispheres.

Be positive and put yourself in a winning attitude.

Plan in a reward; something to look forward to – activity/pastime.

Talk with someone who is reassuring and supportive.

Multi Sense your Work

Decide on the various methods you think will help - read, recite, write, draw, highlight.

If you are attempting a past paper - use all the techniques you have been taught

If it is a timed question - stick to the actual timings and work under the same conditions as you would inthe exam itself.

Overview and In depth study – focus on your objectives throughout.

Half way through include an outstanding item to give yourself a mini break – stretch and brain exercise.

Aim for precision and relevance.

At the end review your work for 5 minutes remember to go over it again later and the following morning – stick to your Review Programme.

At the end of your session

Be clear what you have achieved - what else do you need to do with this topic?

What have you found difficult to understand and do?

Who can you ask for help?

Analyse your next step with the topic; mark it off on your timetable.

Note in your Diary/Organiser what you will have to do next time you go through it.

If necessary, re -schedule your Timetable.

Go and have a good break.

THE ACTIVE ACADEMIC £££££ REWARD OFFERED FOR:

Anyone with these characteristics:

● Knows purpose , what has to be done.

● Summarises work, taking notes properly.

● Listens in class, so homework's easier.

● Uses diagrams, cartoons, colour and symbols to help memory and recall later.

● Uses flow charts, mind maps and diagrams.

● Asks questions about a topic

● Enquiring mind and attitude.

● Produces plans and brief answers to typical questions.

● Recognises that key points/ideas are necessary and waffle isn't.

● Talks to others. Asks for help.

● Teaches others - a great way of revising.

● Uses index cards, revision sheets.

● Records how she is doing.

● Knows how to brainstorm.

● Revises in clever ways.

● Applies work to real life situations.

● Uses a personal organiser to control work and play time.

● Works when brain is most receptive.

● Has a busy social life, is chatty, fun to be with and bright.

Yes ... They do exist !
(Reward = a happy, successful and easier life ahead!)

Use this page to make notes about how you can improve your learning.

Example:

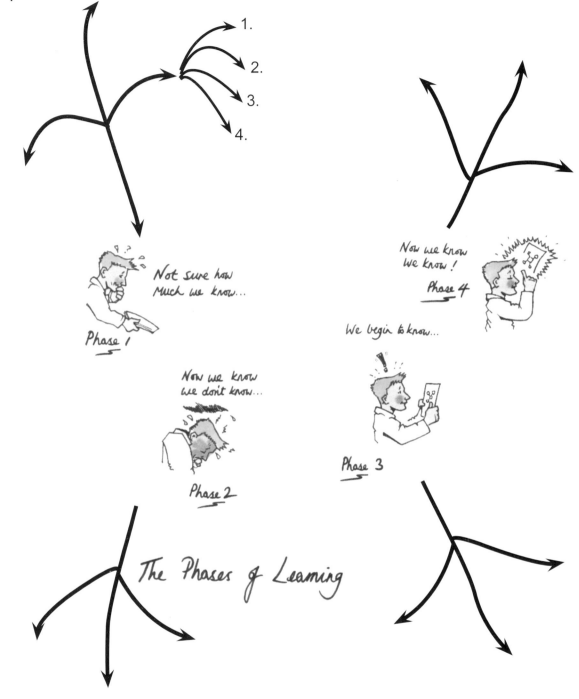

1.

2.

3.

4.

Not sure how Much we know...

Phase 1

Now we know we know! Phase 4

We begin to know...

Now we know we don't know...

Phase 2

Phase 3

The Phases of Learning

See page 18. The 1st Quantum Leap of Lightning Learning.

Use this page to make notes about how you can improve your learning.

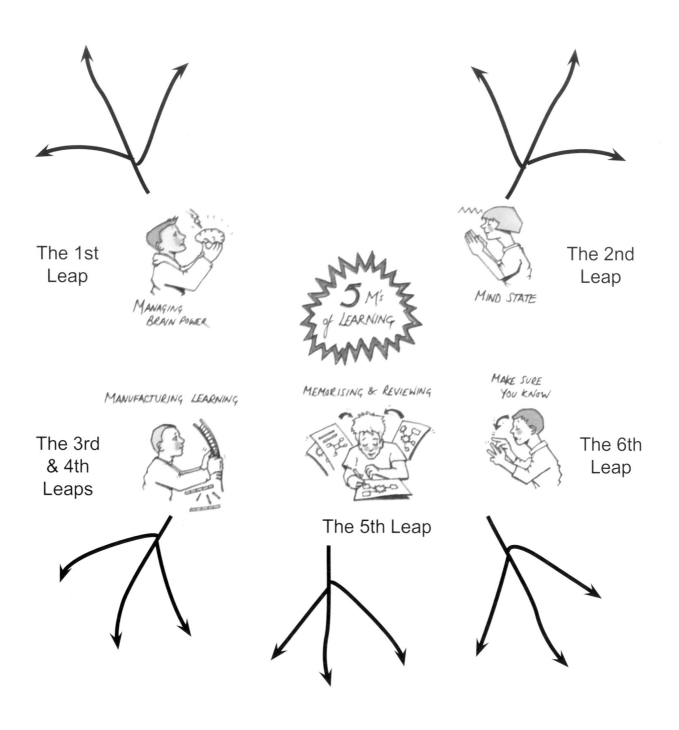

The 1st Leap

MANAGING BRAIN POWER

5 M's of LEARNING

The 2nd Leap

MIND STATE

MANUFACTURING LEARNING

MEMORISING & REVIEWING

MAKE SURE YOU KNOW

The 3rd & 4th Leaps

The 5th Leap

The 6th Leap

See page 19. The 1st Quantum Leap of Lightning Learning.

Use this page to make notes about how you can improve your learning.

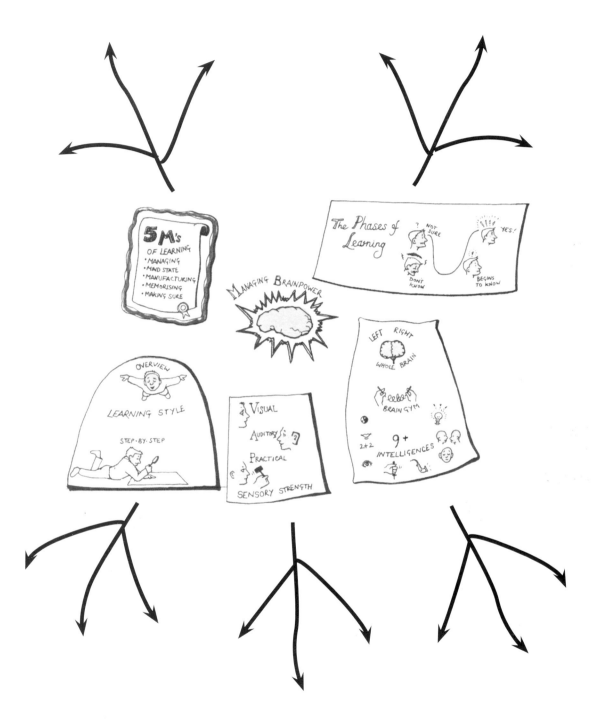

See page 28. The 1st Quantum Leap of Lightning Learning.

Use this page to make notes about how you can improve your learning.

See page 46. The 2nd Quantum Leap of Lightning Learning.

Use this page to make notes about how you can improve your learning.

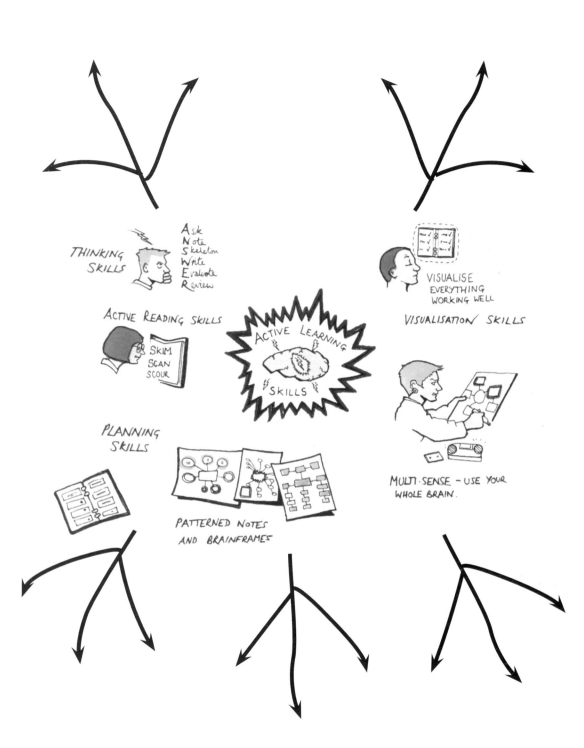

See pages 47, 61 & 69. The 3rd 4th & 5th Quantum Leaps of Lightning Learning.

Use this page to make notes about how you can improve your learning.

See page 95. The 6th Quantum Leap of Lightning Learning.

Use this page to make notes about how you can improve your learning.

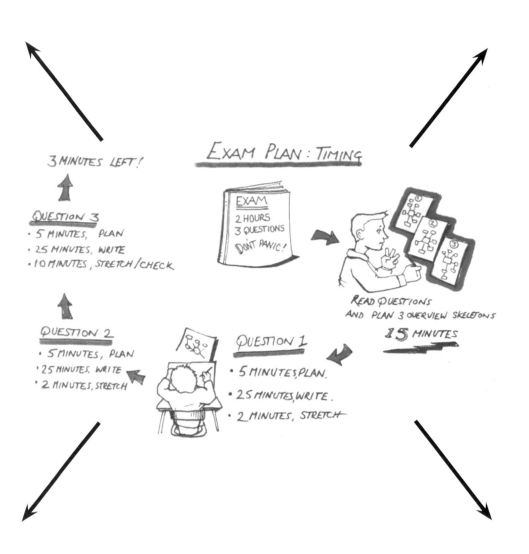

See page 95. The 6th Quantum Leap of Lightning Learning.

Use this page to make notes about how you can improve your learning.

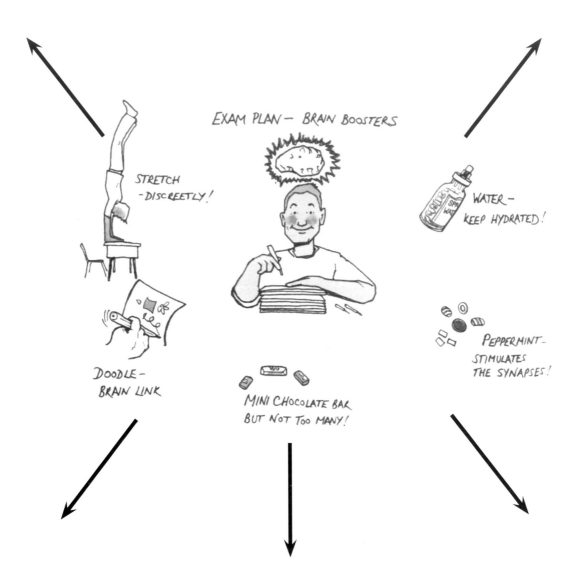

See page 95. The 6th Quantum Leap of Lightning Learning.

Planning Your Time

Look at the cartoon below - what are the study habits she needs to change?

Are you a lousy learner or an active academic?

Answer below:

Are there any habits that are good?

Notes

Time Management

If you know where you time is spent, you should be able to balance what you *have* to do with what you *want* to do.

If you had more **FREE-TIME** wouldn't you be

FREER

MORE FULFILLED

MORE IN CONTROL

HAPPIER

Estimate how much time you spend actually working each day throughout the week	Total for the week
How much time do you spend asleep (officially!), eating, travelling and in general maintaining yourself?	Total for the week
Now deduct the work and maintaining time from 168 (The number of hours in a week.)	Total for the week
How much free time do you have?	Total for the week

How is that time split up each day?
Are you wasting your own time?

WHAT TAKES UP YOUR TIME?
- Sleep
- Work
- Late work
- Re-done work
- Sport
- Art
- Music
- Hobbies/Activities
- Chatting
- Interruptions
- Helping others
- Travel
- Not listening in class
- Visits
- Problems
- Worry

ANY OF THESE FAMILIAR?
- Too much irrelevant detail
- Distractions
- Poor Motivation, self-discipline
- Looking after yourself
- Illness
- Procrastination
- Duties & Responsibilities
- Research
- Family
- Poor Planning
- Not knowing what/why you're studying

A practical guide to Planning your Time.

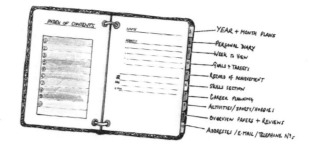

Easy to UNDERSTAND INSTRUCTIONS !

1. Take a piece of paper. Write down your timetable each week – analyse your

    WORK TIME. (lessons, homework)

    MAINTENANCE TIME (sleep wash, rest, travel, etc.)

    FREE TIME (portion per day i.e. ÷ 7)

    Do it
    Delay it
    Drop it

2. Write down "What wastes my time"

3. Work out your **TARGETS** (Aims, objectives ... what you've got to do!)

    for the forthcoming:

    Week   Month Year in order of importance

    (i.e. VITAL! DELAY IT! FORGET IT!)

4. Put them into your   **TIMETABLE / DIARY OR PERSONAL ORGANISER**

5. Make sure to do the TOP PRIORITY ones first

"A's"	"B's"	"C's"
DO IT	DELAY IT	DROP IT
What you must do	What you can do later	What you don't have to do

6. Now you know what's most **URGENT** and **WHEN** you're going to do it.

    So, work out **HOW LONG** you think you'll need on each task

8. Make sure you **STICK TO YOUR PLAN.**

(Lots of students spend hours drawing "State of the Art" plans and timetables ... and then NEGLECT them ... 'All mouth, no action' types.)

Advantages

You're on time.

You're less stressed

Last minute panics are less likely

You'll have more FREE time.

You'll see how you can improve

You'll see how you study best.

You'll feel good!

and.......you'll make progress!

Brain Frame

the 4th leap of lightning learning

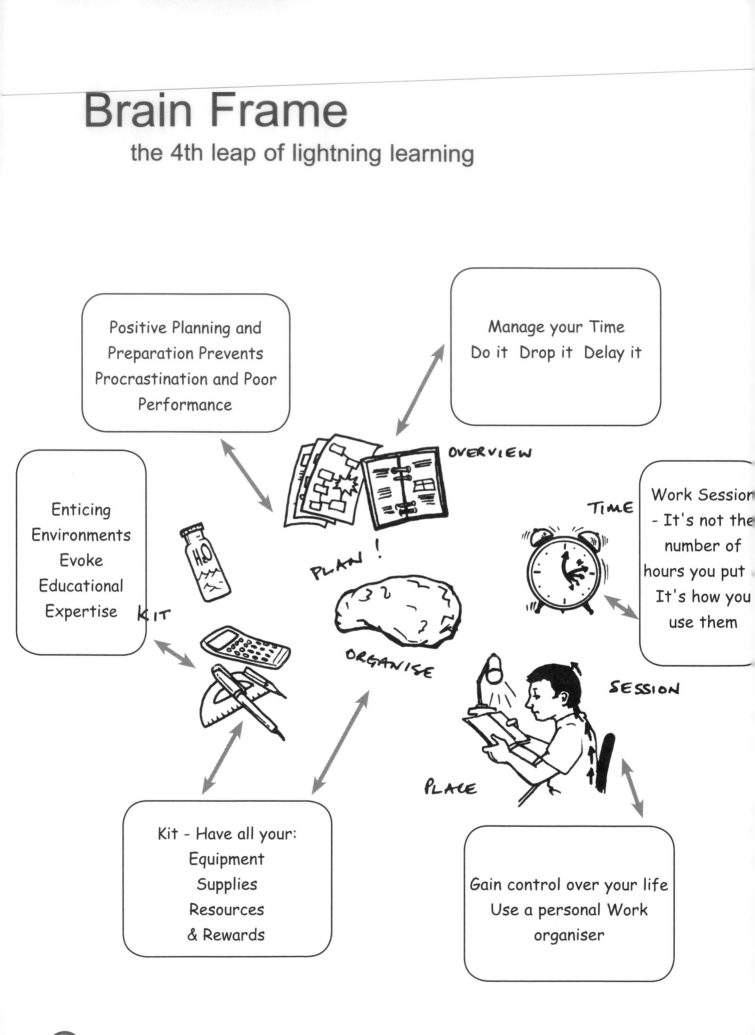

Positive Planning and Preparation Prevents Procrastination and Poor Performance

Manage your Time
Do it Drop it Delay it

OVERVIEW

Enticing Environments Evoke Educational Expertise

PLAN !

ORGANISE

TIME

Work Session - It's not the number of hours you put It's how you use them

SESSION

KIT

PLACE

Kit - Have all your:
Equipment
Supplies
Resources
& Rewards

Gain control over your life
Use a personal Work organiser

Exploring Active Learning

Here we look at active skills that will help you learn in a more 'whole brain' and Multi Sensory manner. As a result you will be able to have more time and better results. You will also have a less pressured, more enloyable life.

You can begin to customise the techniques you use and match them with your dominant learning channel and multi intelligences.

Your learning channels need not always stay the same and you can strenghten them and alter them as you go through life.

In section we will cover:
1. Smart Listening
2. Effective Note taking
3. The Need to Read!
4. The Right Writing of Assignments
5. Using Resources
6. Making Presentations

Look and Learn faster...300%

Notes

Listening

The better you LISTEN, the smarter you'll be;

What is the difference between "hearing" and "listening"? Listening – information is processed by the conscious brain and is remembered; Hearing is not processed, but discarded, unless it is relevant. Here's a acronym to help you remember

L

LINK AND LOCATE. On your way to your lesson try to anticipate what you're studying make yourself mentally prepared – in the right frame of mind. New data is linked to previous information.

I

INDICATORS Listen for the 2/3 themes or objectives that the teacher will introduce early - the main ideas of the lesson/topic

S

SELECTIVE WORDS. These are Key SELECTED words to listen for : "it is vital that". "There are three reasons why ..." "You should consider..." Teachers will also signal these with gestures, pauses and so on.

T

TRY "Body Language." You can be an ACTIVE and a silent listener. It's called Body Language. Be on time. Sit where you can be seen. Join in. Show interest. Your positive body language helps the teacher teach better!

E

ENQUIRE. Ask questions – they clear up any misunderstandings and help you remember what you hear.

N

NOTES. Taking notes is an easy way of concentrating and remembering what you hear. There are many methods; see the Notes section.

LISTEN AND LEARN MORE !

WE ALWAYS HEAR but WE DON'T OFTEN LISTEN

If I listened to myself
more I'd talk less

Note this well!
The Power of Brainframing

Tick or Highlight which apply to you

Do you :

- ❏ Know why note taking is vital?
- ❏ Never take notes?
- ❏ Fail to Plan notes?
- ❏ Copy too much detail? Waste time rewriting again?
- ❏ Waffle - include irrelevant facts?
- ❏ Cram everything onto one page?
- ❏ Ignore layout and presentation (tidiness)?
- ❏ Write everything you're told in long lines of prose?
- ❏ Never use abbreviations? Never use colour?
- ❏ Do you find it impossible to learn from them?
- ❏ Do you forget to file them, lose them?

Note taking saves time and is a memory skill

The skill of note taking is fundamental to your success. We recommend all types of note taking - from linear notes to mind maps or spider diagrams. We especially like the technique of **Brain Framing.**

This involves both the left hemisphere (Lists of logical words, order and sequence) with the right hemisphere (Meaning, colour, shape, pattern and creativity). It means you can still learn groups of related facts and use your fantastic visual memory. You should follow the rules and reasoning below.

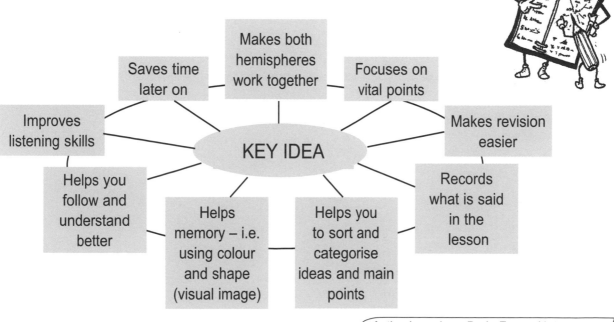

How to make brain frames

Use lots of space

Link ideas

Key ideas / facts only

Once finished, draw a border around

PUT THE MAIN TOPIC IN THE MIDDLE

List related facts.
Give each one a seperate area and frame

Use shorthand abbreviations gvt (omit vowels) dept (omit middle or ending)

Sort ideas and categorise

WHEN

WHY

WHERE

WHAT

WHO

Highlight important words Underline use symbols shapes colours

FLOW DIAGRAM

CHRISTMAS TREE HEADING

FAMILY TREE

HERRING BONE

MIND MAPS

STORY BOARD

Tips when taking notes from texts/books

- Read first - SKIM / SCAN.
- Identify information required; know what you need to know!
- Ask questions.
- Use Post It pads to mark pages ane areas of interest
- Find the main ideas or themes
- Pick key words: use them only
- Record where the information comes from
- Real names/quotations in full
- Leave space for additions
- Don't make it so short or use too many abbreviation so that it makes no sense later!

Make sure that you, so that you can find your notes and information easily:

- file systematically
- have a contents page
- have dividers
- label/number clearly
- use new files/folders
- keep all your files in one place
- keep your notes neat, and re-file occasionally!

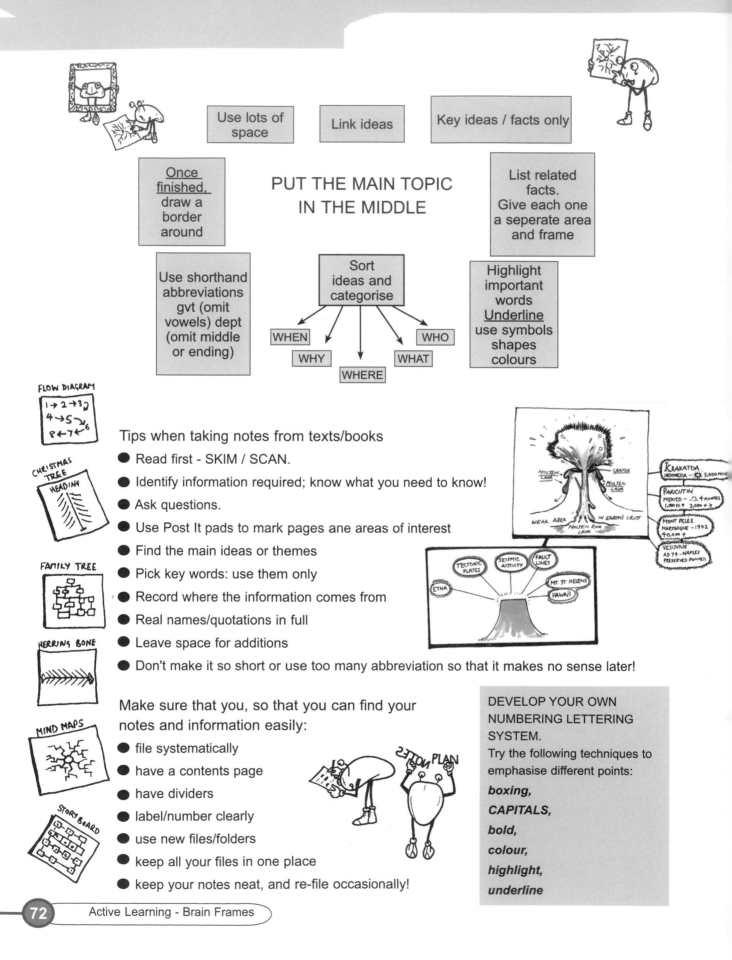

DEVELOP YOUR OWN NUMBERING LETTERING SYSTEM.
Try the following techniques to emphasise different points:

boxing,

CAPITALS,

bold,

colour,

highlight,

underline

The Need to Read

It's vital to be able to *read* according to your need. That's to say that you are able to gain the best information in the shortest possible time - so you don't waste time either reading too much or too little.

Good students will be able to vary what they read according to WHY they have to read it.

Why do students read?

- For pleasure (fun!)
- For practical reasons – instructions and so on. (understanding)
- For general information (general impression – skim through)
- For specific information (fact finding – in depth)
- To learn and memorise (understanding and revision)
- To criticise (making up you own mind, present an argument)
- To detect bias (is the passage one-sided?).
- Because I'm forced to!

Many students waste their own time by using the wrong strategy of reading for their purpose

There are three main strategies of reading something:

SKIMMING: This is gaining a general impression; discovering what the chapter/book is mainly about. Look at first and last paragraphs and first and last sentences.

SCANNING: This is fact finding; looking for specific detail by running your eye down a page fast. Highlight key words.

SCOURING (**DETAILED READING**): This is reading for understanding; information, comprehension and to extract detailed answers.

Always plan before your start, and know your purpose for reading

Why should I have to read this?
How should I start?
What am I looking for?
Therefore, which style of reading do I need for the purpose?

Read according to need

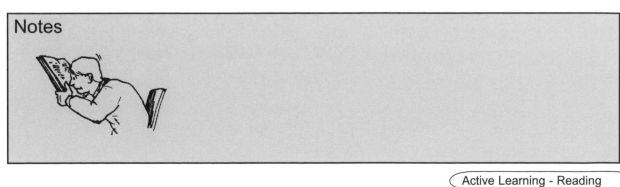

Notes

Improve your Reading Techniques

Understanding memory and speed

1. **Comprehension** is more important than speed.

   (250 - 400 words per minute = good. 500 wpm + excellent. 1000 wpm = YOU'RE A LIAR!)

2. Don't follow words **INDIVIDUALLY**, but in groups. Use punctuation to help.

3. **Try not to mouth words as you read.** (We read 4 times slower this way)

4. **Avoid back-tracking** – when your eyes flick back and re-read subconsciously.

   Follow your reading with a ruler or your finger to stop you.

5. Using a guide can help ... **BUT KEEP IT MOVING.**

6. Some like to use **colour transparent plastic** (often purple/yellow) to stop the

   words jumping or glaring.

7. **Constant practice is vital** (you'll understand more,

   maybe even faster).

8. **Make notes or use a highlighter** – it helps link right and

   left hemispheres and improves understanding.

It always helps to get an overview first. There is no point reading
a whole chapter and not remembering what happened at the
beginning. Read a few paragraphs – go back and check your
understanding

> EXTRA TIPS
>
> You need a non-reflective surface
>
> Good lighting
>
> Read an 18' distance
> (45cm) from page.
>
> Be determined to read
> (set minutes not moments)
>
> Underline, highlight,
> take notes
>
> Every now and then sum up main points.
>
> Sit sensibly
>
> Don't be distracted

S S Q 3 R

To read for Understanding and learning you should use a strategy called SSQ3R:

Skim   Check title & contents. Fast look at pages to get a feel for text
            Chapter headings, Sections, Illustrations & Diagrams.

Scan   Look at index. Fast moving; eyes flicking across page for key
            words/phrases

Question Ask yourself your purpose; what do I want to know?

            Do I need to read it all?

Read   In depth. Find the speed at which you best understand.

            Try to familiarise yourself with specialist vocabulary.

Recall Check understanding. Underline/highlight. Take notes. Test yourself.
            Have you fully answered questions? Is the argument clear?

Review Have you done? What have you learnt?

            How can you improve? You will need to find and concentrate on your weaker areas.

The Right Writing of Assignments

So we've covered a lot, and we have not <u>really</u> discussed what you spend a great deal of time doing: producing written assignments ... for almost every subject.

Such assignments are sometimes called ESSAYS - but there are many other styles of answer such as step-questions, summaries and so forth.

There are 4 writing styles:

FACTUAL   An account based on fact, not opinion

NARRATIVE   A story, perhaps a description; fact, fiction or personal experience.

DISCURSIVE   Discussion/Argument

INVESTIGATIVE   Reports. Experiments. Surveys

So ... How good are you?

Do you know how to   **Tick**

collect good information?   ❏

understand a title?   ❏

organise and plan an answer?   ❏

give enough/relevant detail, without waffling?   ❏

write introductions, developments, conclusions?   ❏

choose the appropriate writing style for the purpose?   ❏

express yourself clearly?   ❏

best present your work?   ❏

be objective (not biased)?   ❏

put forward a well balanced argument or story?   ❏

check your work?   ❏

paragraph, punctuate, spell well?   ❏

writing can be exciting

It will save you time, stress and bring success if you improve these skills.

Notes

Basic Principles of written assignments

Written answers are the result of a problem solving process, you can think of it as a sequence of steps which will need to be taken in order to find a solution and answer the question posed.

STEPS:

1. *What am I being asked to do?*
2. *What do I want to say?*
3. *What information do I need? What do I know already? Brainstorm.*
4. *How do I present it? What is my argument? Visualise it and plan.*
5. *Application. Write it.*
6. *Evaluation: Have I answered the question? How could this be applied to another situation?*

AVOID REPETITION, JARGON, BIAS.

BACK UP POINT WITH FACT, NOT JUST OPINION.

CLEAR HANDWRITING "Can't read, can't mark"!

USE ILLUSTRATIONS/ DIAGRAMS. (Practice them!) They should support evidence, not replace it.

You must CHECK! PROOF READ (Try reading backwards to notice spelling mistakes.)

IMAGINE YOU'RE THE MARKER

Look for the mistakes you know you normally make.

Learn from your mistakes!

Notes

Essay

Here's a mnemonic you can try:

Evaluate the question

What's wanted, what is the question asking you?

Read the question 2 or 3 times to ensure you have the general idea

Rephrase : Is it clear?

What isn't wanted?

Key words - "Command" words, "guide" words

Keep returning to title to help relevance.

Begin at the end - consider your conclusion

Select information and resources

Only relevant material

Short notes

Don't rush

Create links/comparisons

Put in order

Ask yourself : "Is this information useful - is it really needed?"

Sketch and
Structure THE PLAN.

Summary Spidergram.

Linear plans, lists, paragraph headings

INTRODUCTION – Define the queation. Set the scene

DEVELOPMENT – Paragraphs, order, clarity, links. Relevance, balance, opinion, fact

CONCLUSION – Summary, end story

Personal opinion Tie up loose ends

Accurately   WRITE IT

– 1st impressions count.

Write freely. Assume your reader is intelligent.

Paragraphs. Tidy plan = linked points/events.

Clear sentences. Check spelling and puncutation as you go. Use signpost words

Avoid repetition, jargon and bias.

Back up point with fact not just opinion.

Clear handwriting "Can't read, can't mark"!

Use illustartions / programmes. (Practise them!)

Should support evidence, not replace it.

You must proof read

CHECK! PROOF READ

(Try reading backwards to notice spelling mistakes.)

Imagine you're the marker

Look for the mistakes you know you normally make.

LEARN FROM YOUR MISTAKES!

Understanding the Question

These are key words in titles: you must focus on these and know what they mean.

They're called COMMAND words – you should HIGHLIGHT THEM.

KEY WORDS IN TITLES

Account for	Explain and examine the main points
Analyse	Examine component parts
Compare	Look for similarities/differences
Contrast	Set in opposition to bring out differences
Criticise	Judgement of facts or opinion, by reasoned discussion and evidence
Define	Set down precise meaning of a word, phrase, topic
Discuss	Investigate/examine by argument for and against. Debate
Describe	Detailed graphic account
Distinguish/Differentiate	Look for differences between
Enumerate	List or specify and describe
Evaluate	Make an appraisal of worth of something in light of its usefulness
Explain	Make plain. Interpret
Interpret	Make clear and explicit
Illustrate	Make clear and explicit
Justify	Show adequate grounds for decision/ conclusions. Answer objectives
Outline	Give main features/general principals
Prove	Demonstrate truth/falsity with evidence
Relate	Narrate. Show connection between events/facts
Review	Survey. Criticise
State	Present in brief, clean form
Summarise	Concise account of main points omitting detail and examples
Trace	Follow development of topic

ESSAY –

"HISTORY OF THE WORLD"

BY NEXT WEEK

NO EXCUSES !!!

Know the question and the answer is easier

Planning your essay

Sketching your thoughts, ideas and facts into a logical format which you can use as a structure for your essay is probably the most important part of the writing process.

Below are some examples of different planning formats which you might like to try. Choose a format that will fit the style of writing required and which will help answer the question asked.

Plan, action, check = success

Flow Plan   for events and consequences e.g. *Plan a car journey*

Columns   for Argumentative or discursive writing

e.g. Should school uniform be compulsory?

For	Against	Opinion

Brainframe, or Spidergram - Recording All Points

e.g. What are the main features of a volcano?

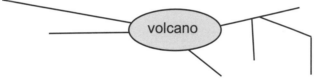

Story Board plan

Introduction	Development
Set Scene	Introduce Characters
Create atmosphere	
Development	
Conclusion Recount events. Tie up loose ends	

Frame
your
brain!

Notes

Write It

Practice makes perfect!
Remember ...
"Can't read -
can't mark."

Some tips to help you write with more confidence and ability

- Keep your handwriting on the line.
- Don't write in a cramped, awkward style.
- Don't write in enormous letters just because you think it will look as though you've written more.

    CLEAR HANDWRITING! "Can't read, can't mark"!

    Practice by writing the following sentence, it contains all the letters of the alphabet:

"The quick brown fox jumps over the lazy dog"

- AVOID REPETITION. JARGON. BIAS.

    Precision and clarity

    Don't be vague.

    What's wrong here? –

"Basically and in general most, if not all, people hate revision, well some do anyhow - and I know this because I read it somewhere some time ago." Avoid generalisations.

- BACK UP POINT WITH FACT, NOT JUST OPINION.

    Be clear. Beware of waffle

    KISS or Keep it simple, stupid! (at least until you're clear in your mind.)

- USE ILLUSTRATIONS/DIAGRAMS. (Practice them!)

    Should support evidence, not replace it.

- CHECK! PROOF READ It is vital to check your work.

    (Try reading backwards to notice spelling mistakes.)

- IMAGINE YOU'RE THE MARKER

    Look for the mistakes you know you normally make.

    Learn from your mistakes

Link Words

These words help you to link your ideas in a logical way

To Begin   "Firstly: the purpose of this report is…."

To add   "Furthermore; moreover; meanwhile; then…"

To illustrate   "For example; to clarify…."

To contrast   "Alternatively, however, on the other hand"

To finish   "To conclude, finally, therefore, thus, ultimately"

REMEMBER

FACTS
Evidence ,information, proven data.

ARGUMENT
Points backed up with proof.

OPINION
Personal beliefs.

Your Essay Review Checklist

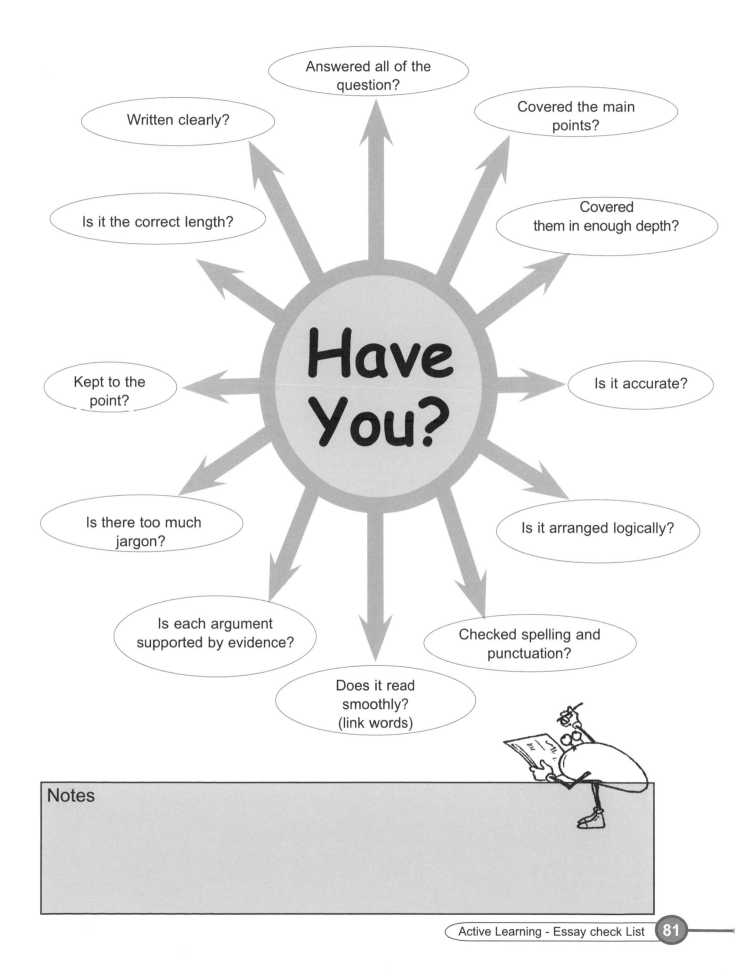

Notes

Using Multi-Sensory Resources

Your approach to work may be holistic (Sky diver) or step by step (Intrepid explorer).

Therefore you should select resources which best suit you way of learning.

Resources include:

    Books - Reference & Text
    Catalogues
    Newspapers
    Videos
    CD ROM
    Slides/Photographs
    TV
    Radio
    Audio Tapes
    Encyclopaedias
    Magazines & Journals
    Libraries & Librarians
    Museums & Galleries

PEOPLE
Don't ignore them –
the information
they have is:
Personal
Real
Immediate
Reassuring
Informative
Often Interesting
Normall Free!

PLACES
There is nothing like
first hand experience

Using resources:

To make use of these resources (perhaps not all at once!) will require some planning and organisation. Too often students rely on a handful of set texts to see them through and they fail to research more widely .

If you are a holistic, visual learner you may want to get an overview first by watching a video before researching specific facts from books. If you are a segmented, auditory learner you may want to interview people and put the pieces together yourself. If you are a physical learner you may prefer to visit museums, experience real situations or try the 'hands on approach'.

Make sure you combine all strategies and use a variety of different resources.

Wise resourcing saves you time!

Notes

Multi Sensory Presentation

Just as you have a preferred learning Channel and learning Approach - so does your reader or Examiner. You should therefore try to present your work in such a way that it appeals to different personalities...

A visual, holistic audience will appreciate an overview with plenty of diagrams, graphs, illustrations in addition to the use of colour, analogies, metaphors and similes.

A step by step reader will appreciate well organised text with skilful use of link words with factual details presented in a consecutive order - perhaps using a numbering system.

All readers appreciate legible handwriting and a tidy, well laid out looking script...

First Impressions are vital

- Use a decent pen - ink or roller ball ; not a cheap biro.
- Vary your presentation according to subjects
- Incorporate where appropriate: pie charts, charts, logs, timelines, bar graphs, diagrams, sketches, annotated maps
- Remember... *"A picture is worth a thousand words"*

Written reports/ projects:

consider...

- Booklets, bound together.
- Typed or hand-written?
- Illustrations. Layout.
- Cover, content, index.

Course work increasingly accounts for a large proportion of total marks... and Presentation is as important as content

Course work checklist

Before you start, check:

- ❏ Do I write on one side or two?
- ❏ Do I use headings or paragraphs?
- ❏ Do I leave a double margin?
- ❏ Name each sheet?
- ❏ Should the title be on each side?
- ❏ Should I use double spacing?
- ❏ Are you supposed to write as: *"I / We . One / You"*?
- ❏ Have you checked for spelling errors?

- ❏ Is typing allowed?
- ❏ Are correction fluids allowed?
- ❏ Should you quote on a separate line?
- ❏ Are diagrams / charts allowed?
- ❏ Should there be a bibliography?
- ❏ Have you proof read it?

Brain Frame

the 5th leap of lightning learning

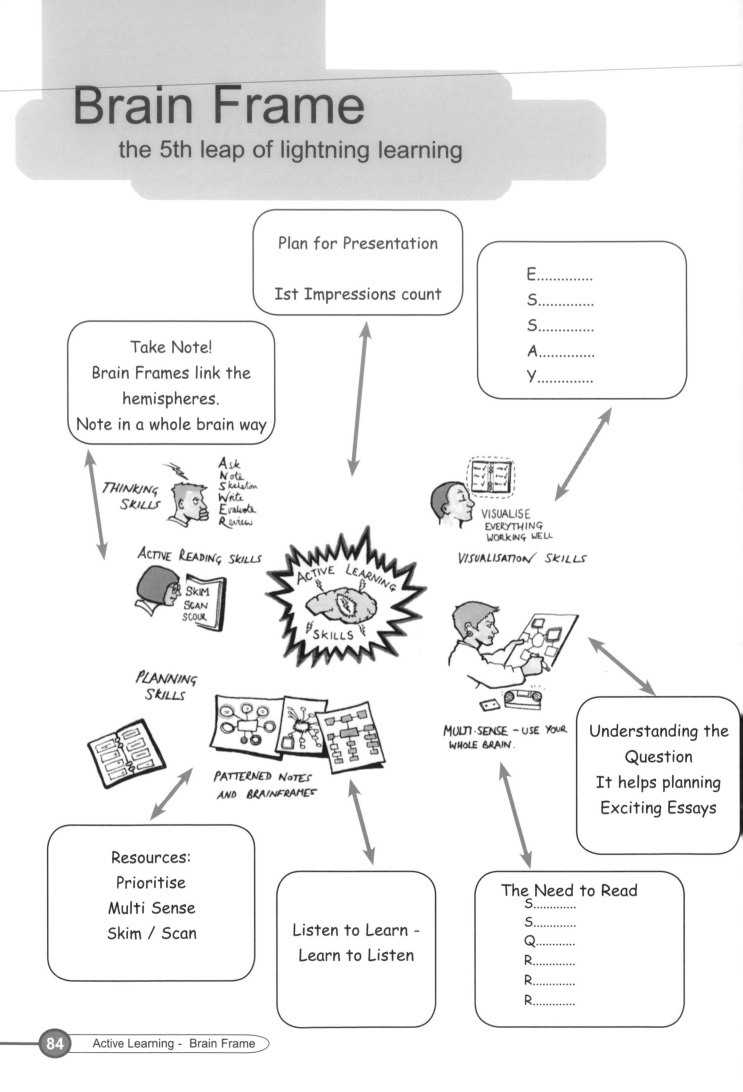

Plan for Presentation

Ist Impressions count

E.............
S.............
S.............
A.............
y.............

Take Note!
Brain Frames link the
hemispheres.
Note in a whole brain way

THINKING SKILLS

Ask
Note
Skeleton
Write
Evaluate
Review

ACTIVE READING SKILLS

SKIM SCAN SCOUR

ACTIVE LEARNING SKILLS

VISUALISE EVERYTHING WORKING WELL

VISUALISATION SKILLS

PLANNING SKILLS

PATTERNED NOTES AND BRAINFRAMES

MULTI·SENSE – USE YOUR WHOLE BRAIN.

Understanding the
Question
It helps planning
Exciting Essays

Resources:
Prioritise
Multi Sense
Skim / Scan

Listen to Learn -
Learn to Listen

The Need to Read
S.............
S.............
Q.............
R.............
R.............
R.............

The Sixth Leap into Lightning Learning

Memory, Revision and Exams. Show You Know

Introduction

Once you have mastered your learning approach, style, motivation and organisation ... you'll be a "whole brain" learner. Now you need to show you know. This involves the power to use your memory well under pressure. Once you have learned how to Review your work (revision) you will find tests and exams easier.

In section we will cover:

1. Memory and Learning Strategies

2. Effective and Active Revision Planning

3. Exam Preparation and

4. Exam Techniques for Success

I used to have a good memory – but I can't remember when

Notes

Memory

What is Memory?

Memory is the ability to encode, store and retrieve information.

All learning depends upon memory – without it everything we do would be a new experience.

How does the Memory Work?

There are 3 parts - 1. Your Sensory (VAP) receptors

2. STM = Short term memory – the holding centre for 7 facts.

3. LTM = Long term memory – the permanent filing cabinet

Messages are first encoded by the STM which holds up to 7 pieces of information. These have to be transferred to the LTM by rehearsal in the working memery by the inner voice (repeating) or the inner eye (or visualising or doing). If the information is not rehearsed it will be lost or replaced by new information within seconds.

Reheasal

| Incoming Information | → | Sensory Register | → | Short-term Memory | → | Long-term Memory |

The transfer of information to the LTM involves chemical reactions (remember the process of myelination: neuron back roads become neurone highways?) The more you practise the more automatic it becomes and the quicker messages travel.

There is a great deal that still needs to be discovered about how memory works. But we do know that the more you use your memory the more efficient it becomes.

You also have a Visual, Auditory and Motor memory stores which is why you should learn in a *Multi-Sensory* way and use them all to make as many different connections in your brain as you can.

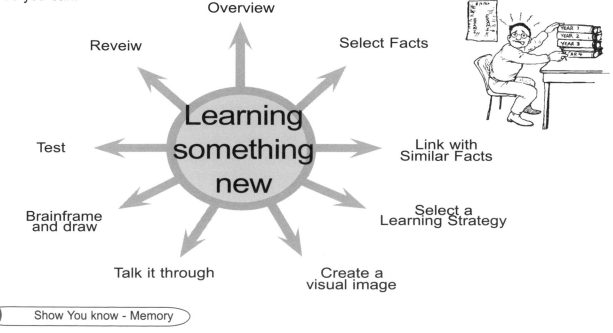

Overview

Reveiw

Select Facts

Test

Link with Similar Facts

Learning something new

Brainframe and draw

Select a Learning Strategy

Talk it through

Create a visual image

Why do we forget

1. Poor understanding. Your Long Term Memory will not encode information it does not understand.

2. Poor reception. Poor attention, poor listening, lack of interest or attention.

3. Distractions. When your mind is on other problems, such as an exciting event or relationships.

4. Your physical state. Tiredness, anxiety, emotions, mood and stress will interfere with encoding.

5. Interference. New information being confused with existing information – for example when you learn similar things together without proper consolidation. (French Revolution followed by Russian Revolution)

6. Repression. Unpleasant experiences (i.e. failure in a subject) will inhibit learning of that subject.

7. Poor Learning Strategy, not having cues or memory triggers to unlock and retrieve the facts.

8. Insufficient Rehearsal or Practice to consolidate information. Not having a Review Cycle.

9. Lack of importance: You don't remember the unimportant (You probably don't remember what you had for supper last Wednesday - you do remember what presents you were given last birthday!)

10. Improper organisation when you are learning: trying to cram in too much information into your memory filing cabinet without sorting it into categories.

11. Disuse. Over time myelin breaks down and connections are lost.

12. De-Hydration the brain needs plenty of water to conduct electrical pulses fast.

13. Stress – feeling anxious closes down access to the Thinking Brain.

TRY THIS

In a relaxed and focused moment try to learn the following (allow two minutes):

1: Car	6: Green	11: Salt	16: Love
2: Honesty	7: CD	12: Cart	17: Stero-system
3: Chips	8: Bicycle	13: Hate	18: Plane
4: Black	9: Revenge	14: Calculator	19: Vinegar
5: Computer	10: Fish	15: Yellow	20: Red

What did you learn from the exercise?

Did you use any methods to help you remember?

See next page...

Remembering

Rules and Conditions

Remember,
relax . . .
see it,
hear it,
speak it,
do it

Create Interest. Find a purpose. "Why is this useful?"

Understand it. It's impossible to learn what you don't understand.

Positive Thinking and Confidence. Sometimes we fail to learn because we convince ourselves we can't do it. "I WILL REMEMBER"

Intend to attend to it! Be determined to learn - avoid distractions.

Rehearse out aloud. Speak it aloud. – Create a script. Verbalise.

Create Visual Images. We learn much better what we can picture in our mind's eye or see in a diagram, chart or photograph.

Organise information. Organise into sensible "chunks" and rehearse. Do not try to learn too much at once - 7 items.

Create Associations. It's much easier to learn new things that you can link to something you already know.

Remember the 'Unusual'. If something is funny, strange, spooky, bizarre or even rude it's more memorable.

Develop a System. Use memory triggers for each item you want to remember. For example, a souvenir will trigger endless holiday memories.

Use a Multi Sensory approach Employ a combination of audio, visual and physical strategies to use your visual audio and motor memories.

Be Relaxed. Play non lyrical music to help the Beta waves buzz.

Plan ahead. Plan what you want to learn.

Make your facts varied and interesting. Use colour, charts, diagrams, drawings, brain frames, flash cards, tape recordings, posters.

Involve your Emotions. You will remember better what makes you feel happy, amused, successful and praised.

Remember best the information you receive beginning and end of a work session. Try having a very short change in the middle of a work session to create a false ending and beginning. This called an Outstanding Item Study for a maximum of 40 minutes, then break.

Memory Exercise from previous page:

If you've just tried the exercise on the last page, you might have made some observations:

Categories...

Visualising...

Your senses....all help you to remember

And, that you remember the first

and last words best!

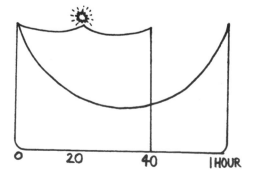

OUTSTANDING ITEM

Learning Strategies

TO CHECK LEARNING
one hour: review
one day: review
one week: review
one month: review
three month: review
and so on . . .

Mnemonic
Using the initial letter to create a sentence.
'Richard Of York Gave Battle In Vain'.
Red Yellow Green Blue Indigo Violet
(Spectrum of the rainbow)

Rhyming mnemonic, poem or lyrics
'30 Days hath September'...
Chant, make up a song, rap

Create a story or movie in your mind
Use visual imagery and verbalise.
(Talk your way through it, to yourself or a friend).

Associate ideas Carbon dioxide - Car engines - Greenhouse effect -Trees - Photosynthesis - Carbon dioxide.

Repeat and test
Look, cover, write, say, check

Look for meaning in what you know already
Neuron (Brain Cell) = neurotic = nervous disorder

Compare with what you know already
How do plant cells differ from animal cells?

The Location or Room System
Assign places/objects around your room to key facts

Visualise
the room and the facts return too!

Number rhymes
'1 = BUN   2 = SHOE   3 = TREE   4 = DOOR'

Brainframes, posters, charts
Hang them round your room – for sub conscious learning

Doodle, highlight, cartoon, underline
Make key ideas and facts stand out

Use a tape
Record ideas and listen when you are relaxing.

Use concrete materials
Build it to represent what is happening

Memory Triggers
Associate the facts with something
unusual or bizarre

Use Flash Cards
For brain frames and key ideas .

Chunk and categorise
Ideas into sequence and groups.

Multi-Sensory Memory

Chunks

Visualise

Highlight

Colour

Brainframes

Links

Categories

Sequences

Repeat and test

Flash cards

7 Facts/ideas

Regular breaks

Teach others

Receive

Rehearse

Retain

Retrieve

Review

Effective Revision

How good are you now?

Please tick the following if they apply to you:

(Think of your last exam...)

YOU'VE BEEN REVISING ALL ALONG!

☐ I looked through the syllabus and checked I covered each topic.

☐ I made a detailed revision timetable several weeks before the exam

☐ I find it difficult to stick to my Revision Timetable.

☐ I began to revise too late.

☐ I read everything from start to finish.

☐ I copied and learnt my notes word for word.

☐ I stayed up late the night before the exam.

☐ I revised the topics I knew best as it was easier.

☐ I put off revising difficult topics.

☐ It was hard to memorise facts and figure

☐ I worked through past papers.

☐ I knew where, when and how long each exam was.

☐ I worked with key ideas and facts.

☐ I worried a lot.

> If any of the above seem familiar...you're right...It's Lightning Learning and if you've been sticking to it... you've been Revising all the time!

Steps towards effective revision:

■ Timetable and Organisation

■ Planning each session

■ Conditions /Environment

■ Memory

■ Note making

■ Smart Reading

■ Finding a purpose

■ Past Papers

■ Testing & 'contract studying'

■ Rewards

■ Fitness

■ Worry

■ All work and no play?

Use Variety, Attitude and Mind State

IF YOU'VE BEEN WORKING TO THE 7 STEPS OF LIGHTNING LEARNING -

YOU'VE BEEN REVISING ALL ALONG!

Revision Timetable and Review Plan

The importance of a Timetable should not be underestimated:

You should have a LONG TERM TIMETABLE (Monthly).

You can mark on it EVERYTHING you have to do including which subjects you intend to revise and on which days.

You should have a LIST of all topics for each subject (see your teacher - and don't leave any out).

You should identify those topics you know best and prioritise the others.

You should have a WEEKLY timetable - mark on it when you intend to revise, work normally and relax: fill in topics per day.

You should tick each TOPIC when you have revised it - and you should review each topic at least 3 times.

You should build in EMERGENCY SPARE TIME: a period each day - "flexitime" - when you can catch up or relax if you've done well.

The Timetable

m			
t			
w			

The Place

It must be quiet, organised, light, ventilated.

Use a desk and chair that match each other in height.

Have all the equipment and resources you need ready, before you start.

Use a memory review system & timetable

A revision timetable is essential. Monthly, weekly and session by session. Start early enough and you will be able to cover every topic often enough. Have a syllabus checklist to keep control of your progress.

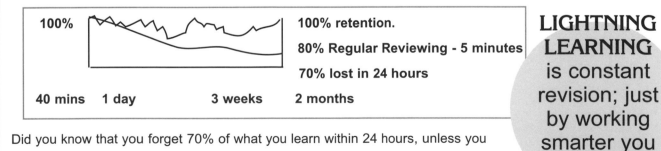

100%	100% retention.
	80% Regular Reviewing - 5 minutes
	70% lost in 24 hours
40 mins 1 day 3 weeks 2 months	

LIGHTNING LEARNING is constant revision; just by working smarter you learn better and faster

Did you know that you forget 70% of what you learn within 24 hours, unless you rehearse it regularly? Try reviewing just before you sleep and just after you wake up.

If you regularly review you will keep up to 80% retention.

Your learning time can be halved. Review your work in many different ways.

Should I cram?

In short, NO!

1. Fast in, fast out = Memory overload.

2. Exam exhaustion – you become "battle weary" after a few days and memory goes!

3. When you cram you don't have the overall view.

4. Cramming means you left it too late and this is de-motivating·

"Study Contracts"

Formally agree your Study Rules

Many people work in pairs, especially when revising.

There are many advantages:

> Improved memory work
>
> Shared labour ideas
>
> Motivation and more time saved
>
> Teaching someone else is a
>
> great way to learn

There are also disadvantages:

> Working together can be a distraction
>
> Choosing the wrong partner
>
> Using it as an excuse to play rather than work
>
> One works, the other copies... so it's a waste of time

So ... agree a proper study contract.

Stress & Anxiety

Do you worry about Exams?

This is called STRESS and can cause panic.

You feel you can't cope.

How do you deal with it ?

Plan ahead, balance work and play

Relax well

Constructive "self-talk"

Plan in rewards

Try to predict the "tough times"

Keep fit/sleep well/good diet

Start revising early

Talk and ask for help

(see page 38)

Notes

Active Revision

***First consider how best to revise
a subject or topic.***

What do I know already?

What do I need to know?

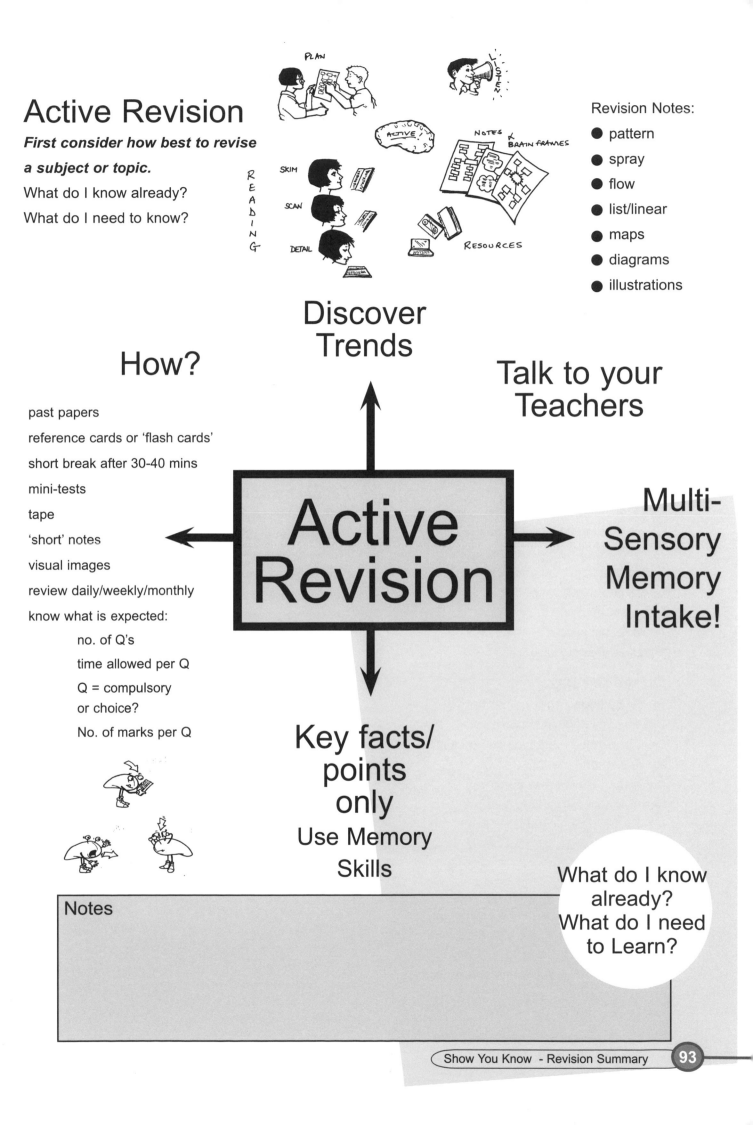

Revision Notes:

- pattern
- spray
- flow
- list/linear
- maps
- diagrams
- illustrations

Discover Trends

How?

past papers

reference cards or 'flash cards'

short break after 30-40 mins

mini-tests

tape

'short' notes

visual images

review daily/weekly/monthly

know what is expected:

    no. of Q's

    time allowed per Q

    Q = compulsory
    or choice?

    No. of marks per Q

Active Revision

Talk to your Teachers

Multi-Sensory Memory Intake!

Key facts/ points only
Use Memory Skills

What do I know already?
What do I need to Learn?

Notes

Exams

Exam Preparation

What exam?

Which exam, when is it?

Where is it?

How long does it last?

How many questions and how long for each?

Mark allocation?

(See past papers: ask how they are marked.)

The day before; THE DAY

Don't revise late.

Don't try to learn new material.

Check through (skim/scan) notes/

Typical Q's?

Collect all equipment you need.

Check your watch works.

Relax before going to bed.

Avoid "panic people".

Visualise your success.

On the Big Day:

Reaffirm venue.

Get up early enough to wake up!

Drink water and eat a high energy meal.

Arrive in good time.

(too early – others may panic you:

exactly on time – can feel late.

(Just a few minutes before is fine.)

If you're delayed – still turn up.

Equipment

Check you have enough pens, pencils,

colours, rubber, ruler, maths equipment,

calculator, any texts you're allowed, dictionary,

lucky mascot?

Make sure your watch works and is accurate.

The Exam Day

The Exam Room

Check your desk and chair

is steady and comfortable.

Relax, calm down take a few deep breaths

Think positively – believe in yourself.

If in doubt about anything - ask the invigilator.

Try brain exercises to link hemispheres

Follow Instructions

Listen to the invigilator. (There can be changes.)

Read written instructions carefully.

(These can be altered.)

Fill in exam. Centre details. Name. Number page.

Read all questions. Eliminate,

Choose very carefully.

Think about a general plan.

Planning. Timing & Technique

Read the questions 2/3 times – slowly

Remember how you've been advised to plan the exam

How much:

   Reading time

   Planning time

   Time for each answer

   Checking time

   Draw up a plan –

   perhaps in a pie chart format

EXAMS:
The chance to
SHOW you
KNOW!

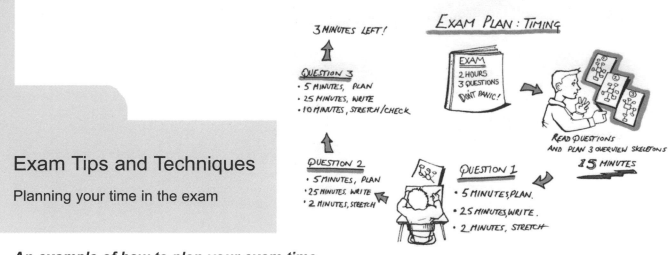

Exam Tips and Techniques

Planning your time in the exam

An example of how to plan your exam time

9.15 – 9.30	Read & choose your questions
9.30 – 9.40	Plan
9.40 – 10.10	Q 1
10.10 – 10.40	Q 2
10.40 – 11.10	Q 3
11.10 – 11.15	Check through
Total: 2 hours	

What can happen if you don't plan your time?

- You rush answers.
- You panic.
- You leave answers out.
- You miss obvious questions.
- Your memory doesn't react.

What happens if you fall behind in your plan?

- Don't panic: reduce each answer time.
- Go into **NOTE** form if absolutely necessary.
- Finish **EACH** question.

PLAN YOUR
READING TIME:
Reading
Planning
Answering
Checking

Planning the answer:

Choose the style of plan you want to use, it doesn't matter which. You can use brainframes, linear plans, flow diagrams.

Try to put across your point in an ordered, logical way – planning well should help.

Look for KEY WORDS in questions - "Guide/signal" words.

What do they want?

Build in checking time.

EXAM PLAN: ANXIETY MANAGEMENT

VISUALISE

CONTROL YOUR BREATHING

STRETCH

MAKE OVERVIEW SHEETS

DRINK WATER

What is a "Good Answer"?

A good answer......

- Comes from a well revised topic.
- Is the result of a well understood question.
- Is often anticipated in revision.
- Is planned carefully.
- Is relevant (sticks to the question, no waffle).
- Is clearly written & makes sense.
- Is presented well, and has all the necessary.
- Is produced in the way you've been taught.
- Is finished.
- Is checked.
- Pleases you!

What Happens if my Mind Goes Blank and I Panic?

I can't do any of these!

Relaxation techniques do help.

Massage your neurovascular points.

Focus your breathing – take big breaths.

Panic/anxiety only lessens your chances of choosing the right question or point.

Don't spend too long trying to remember a point – leave a space/line.

Come back.

Keep writing even on rough paper.

Any ideas/thoughts. Ask yourself questions.

See the invigilator if it becomes worse.

You should have had plenty of practice at this by the time you sit your exam!

Cheating Doesn't Pay

Believe it or not - some people really set out to fool the examiner by "cribbing".

You may have tried it in class tests – but what does it tell you?

You haven't done the work.

You gain marks you don't deserve

How would you feel when others don't do as well, but perhaps deserved to do
better than you.

What reaction would you get from others if they knew?

How would you feel if you knew others had cribbed and did better than you?

It tells you that you're not really up to the standard required.

All good reasons for doing the right thing!

Post Mortems

Is a 'post mortem' a good idea?

Should you go through an exam immediately afterwards to assess your success rate?

On the plus side, you could get plenty of reassurance if you've done well!

On the other hand, if you discover you've done badly you will be highly de-motivated and it
might affect your performance in other exams.

Don't look back – look forward!

Summary
Remember this exam acronym

High Scores

Have faith in yourself   *(Confidence. Positive Thinking. Do your best.)*
Investigate in advance   *(Know topics. Types of Q. Venue. Timings.)*
Govern your preperation   *(Revise positively and actively.)*
Have ideas   *(Be proactive: anticipate and be creative in your revision.)*

Sort out question times   *(Plan each exam, each question.)*
Check approach and guide words   *(Define the question. Read 2/3 times. Look for signal words.) Be careful to choose the best - those that will gain you the highest marks.)*

Organise your plans   *(Read each question carefully and mentally plan your answers. Produce a proper plan. Be sure you can answer/finish it.)*

Recall   *The KEY facts ,ideas or points so you have the Skeleton of an answer*

Engage in the answer   *Write answer. Check for relevance, clarity, presentation as you go along*

Save marks   *(Proof-read content. Punctuation. Relevance. Spelling. Save marks!)*

Brain Frame
the 6th leap of lightning learning

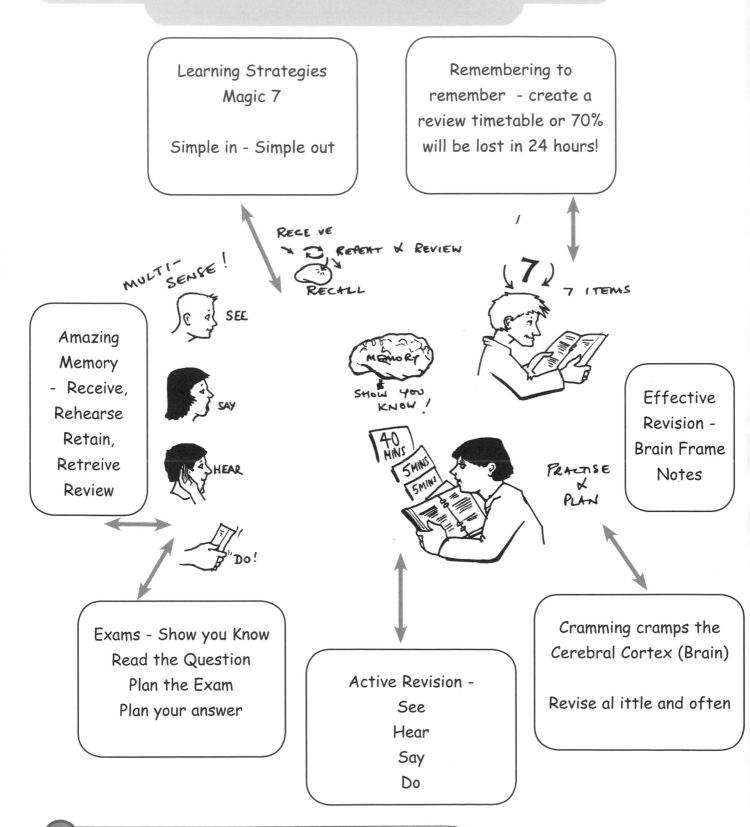

Learning Strategies
Magic 7

Simple in - Simple out

Remembering to
remember - create a
review timetable or 70%
will be lost in 24 hours!

Amazing
Memory
- Receive,
Rehearse
Retain,
Retreive
Review

MULTI-SENSE!

RECE.VE

REPEAT & REVIEW

RECALL

SEE

SAY

HEAR

"DO!"

MEMORY

SHOW YOU KNOW!

40 MINS

5 MINS

5 MINS

7

7 ITEMS

PRACTISE & PLAN

Effective
Revision -
Brain Frame
Notes

Exams - Show you Know
Read the Question
Plan the Exam
Plan your answer

Active Revision -
See
Hear
Say
Do

Cramming cramps the
Cerebral Cortex (Brain)

Revise al ittle and often

The Positive Progress Process

As with all good learning you need to constantly review it. This section helps you maintain a positive focus on your progress.

In section we will cover:

1. Recording your progress

2. How to create an Action Plan

3. Learning from your mistakes

4. Catch yourself doing it 'right'

5. Create your own customised Learning Approach

6. Reflecting upon your learning

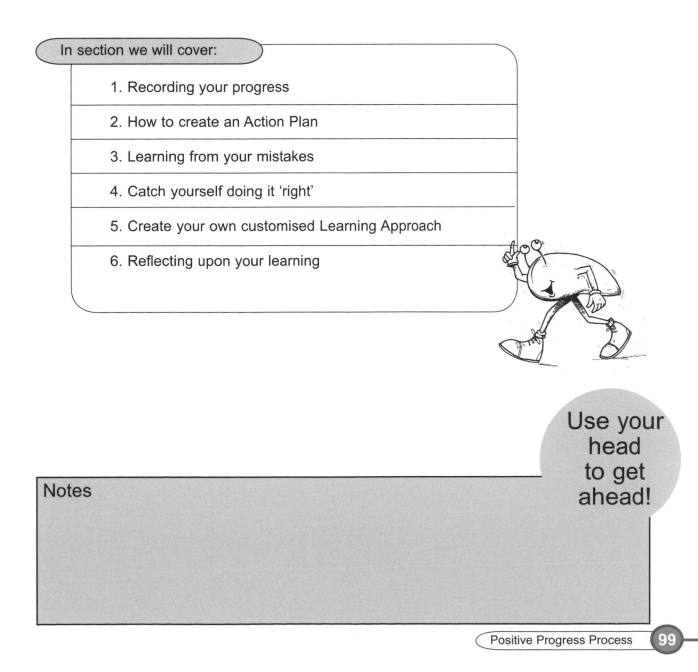

Use your head to get ahead!

Notes

THE POSTIVE

	Yes	Partly	No

The 1st Leap

I understand my brain is divided into three parts

I recognise I need to be relaxed to study well

I understand that my mood and emotions influence my learning

I understand that my Higher thinking brain is divided into two halves, Right and Left
 and that each is responsible for different skills

I recognise I have a Learning approach - I'm either a holistic or a sequential learner

I know I have three main channels for learning – Visual, Auditory and Tactile/Physical

I can learn Consciously and Sub Consciously using my Alpha, Beta, Theta waves

I know I learn best in a Multi Sensory way, using all my intelligences and
 that this will link both brain hemispheres and rapidly increase my learning.

I know what has worked/not worked for me in the past

I can increase the number of connections between brain cells by studying in a
 Multi sensory way.

The 2nd Leap

I understand how important my state of mind is to my Learning success.

I know I'm responsible for my personal development

I recognise the difference between positive and negative attitudes

I know that having a positive attitude will help me go further in my studies and life

I know I can remove the restricting self beliefs I have had about learning in the past.

I know how to motivate myself

I understand how important it is to set goals (work and play)

I understand how important Purpose and Value are in Learning

I understand how vital it is to be in control of my stress levels

The 3rd Leap

I understand what Intelligence means and I understand I have 8 good Intelligences

I have a good idea of which Intelligence's are my best

I understand that intelligence is not 'fixed' for life !

I know that using Multi sensory/Global intelligence techniques will help my success!

The 4th Leap

I understand how important it is to plan and organise my time

workplace

equipment

work session

I recognise that long-term, mid-term and short-term goals are important

I recognise that goals become targets, and targets become tasks

I know how to concentrate better

The 5th Leap

I understand how important it is to have an overview of a subject

I can work out how and where to begin studying a subject

I know how to listen properly

I know how to take notes when reading or listening

I know how to skim or scan a text

I understand my purpose for reading

I know how to stop and check I'm understanding what I'm learning

I realise the need to concentrate on key words, facts, ideas

I recognise the importance of 'visualising' what I'm learning

I see the importance of patterned, colourful Brainframes

I understand how to interpret questions

I understand how to plan answers

I understand how to make the most of illustrations (charts, diagrams, etc.)

I know how important it is to talk with others and work well in groups

I file my work properly as it's easy to find

I know what 'resources' are and how to find them

I know how to improve my 'exciting writing'

The 6th Leap

I understand how my memory works

I understand how I forget

I recognise how important it is to repeat learning regularly
(within 24 hrs, 1 week etc.)

I realise how important it is to create the right conditions for memorising

I understand the 'rules' of memory

I know how important revision timetables are

I recognise how dangerous cramming is

I know how I can create my best Revision style and approach

I understand what 'examinations' really involve

I know how to control exam nerves, mind blanks etc

I realise how important it is to plan each exam

I know how important it is to proof-read each exam

The 7th Leap

I recognise how important it is to have an Action Plan

I recognise how important it is to have a Progress Check

I recognise how important it is to keep positive

I recognise that my attitude will determine altitude in life

I recognise that I should 'catch myself getting it right!'

I recognise that success breeds success!

I recognise that I can and will do it!

Yes Partly No

My Action Plan

Go back through each of the 7 Leaps and pick ideas, suggestions and techniques that appeal to you. Use them to create at least three objectives that you intend to achieve for each of the sections below.

My Unique Brain :

My State of Mind :

My Multi – Sensory Learning :

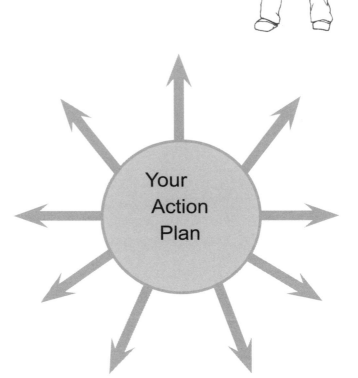

My Organisation and Planning :

My Active Learning :

My Memory, Revision and Exam Skills :

Check back to the end of each Leap .... The Brainframe will help you to remember

Reflective Thinking

Understanding Self-Reflection

"I can't tell you what you are.....You can't tell me what I see!"

The purpose of reflection is to review your learning to be aware of new possibilities and opportunities

"If you continue to do what you've always done, then you'll continue to get what you've always got!"

✓ Don't leave this until some problem forces you to take a close look at yourself. Make it a part of your daily and weekly development process.

✓ Reflection is also very positive if you share your thoughts with a learning partner, friend, mentor or others in a similar learning situation. You can check and gain re-assurance about your perception and analysis - gain others ideas and discuss immediate feedback.

✓ What are my current tasks in daily life?

✓ What are my important strengths?

✓ What are my major weaknesses?

✓ What skills am I good at?

✓ What do I enjoy doing in work and life?

✓ What problems are there in my work/life?

✓ What have been my major achievements?

✓ What have I been disappointed about?

Getting feedback from others is very important, but it can be a lively experience! The way you receive any feedback is important.

Bear this in mind:

Do: ask people you trust and respect for feedback

Do: be honest and open

Do: remember that face-to-face feedback is best, however difficult

Do: ask questions - Who? When? Why? How? What?

Do: listen fully to answers or comments

Do: focus on specific issues you want to know about

Don't: be too quick to judge. Keep an open mind

Don't: make excuses for answers or comments given

Don't: don't look as though you resent it

Don't: argue. Accept opinion and consider them later

Now discuss this feedback with your 'learning' supporter. This will aid clarity and fair judgement. You're still in control - it will be up to you to alter / adapt if you need to

And finally...

Remember ...

You can learn from your mistakes.

Mistakes are simply 'what you're going to get right next time' - they're not failures, but opportunities for success.

but ... prevention is better than cure !

Catch yourself getting it right !

Success comes in cans - not cannots. Beware of how good you really are.

Don't concentrate the negatives, but the positives.

You're unique and very capable.

Record every success, however small.

Your attitude will determine your altitude...in life.

The way you feel about your learning is the most important

aspect of your success. Try to be positive

Creating my own Customised Plan is the secret!

It's your life - Your responsibility.

Remember - "only the best for the best "

You can't blame others, because only ***you*** have the power to make yourself succeed, so go on and empower yourself!

You can use your head to get ahead.

Your ideal Whole Brain Learning, using Multi – Sensory methods and skills is truly global learning.

By combining conscious and sub-conscious learning you'll be way ahead!

Lightning Learning

This text has shown you how to create the conditions, opportunities and systems for you to excel and achieve success, not just with your learning and studying. It has also revealed that these are life skills that you can employ in everything you do!

It's the NEW YOU !

Every time you start towards a new goal, you're already succeeding !

It's the Upwardly Mobile Success Spiral !

And Good Luck!

But you won't depend upon luck alone, will you?